Advance comments on *The Gentle Smile*...

"Diane Berke is a wonderful teacher and writer whose voice and message ought to be widely heard. Drawing from a depth and breadth of spiritual tradition and teaching, rich in its own wisdom and warmth, her work is a unique contribution to all of our hearts. The Gentle Smile is a spiritual gem — an intelligent and heart-opening guide to becoming a more peaceful, loving human being. I recommend it wholeheartedly to anyone seeking to live a happier, wiser, more meaningful life."

—MARIANNE WILLIAMSON, author, *Return to Love, Illuminata,* and *A Woman's Worth*

"I celebrate Diane's commitment to teaching higher truths. She is a light that illuminates my life. I love her work and quote her frequently."

—DR. WAYNE DYER, author, *Everyday Wisdom, Your Erroneous Zones,* and *You'll See It When You Believe It*

"Within moments of meeting Diane I sensed I had met a truly exceptional teacher. Whether through her writings or the blessing of her presence, Diane's love, wise counsel, humor, and unfailing compassion are a gift to all who are touched by her."

—ROBIN CASARJIAN, author, *Forgiveness: A Bold Choice for a Peaceful Heart*

"Diane is a masterful, heart-centered teacher of miracle living. I find her loving wisdom a powerful tool to remember heaven even as I walk the earth."

—ALAN COHEN, author, *The Dragon Doesn't Live Here Anymore, Rising in Love,* and *The Peace That You Seek*

"Diane has a way of grounding spirituality in real experience and in the disciplined work of honestly facing ourselves. Her writing is a blend of clarity and practicality that helps people go deeper in their spiritual process rather than drift into denial, avoidance wishful or mere positive thinking."

—POLLY BERRIEN BERENDS, author, *Coming to Life*

"I deeply appreciate Diane's work."

—KEN KEYES, JR., author, *The Power of Unconditional Love, Handbook to Higher Consciousness,* and *Prescriptions for Happiness*

"Diane is deeply devoted to her spiritual awakening. Her willingness to listen for and follow love's inner urgings and her ability to share her process with others are beautiful gifts to us all."

—LEE COIT, author, *Listening,* and *Listening...Still*

The
Gentle
Smile

The Gentle Smile

Practicing Oneness
in Daily Life

Diane Berke

CROSSROAD · NEW YORK

1995

The Crossroad Publishing Company
370 Lexington Avenue, New York, NY 10017

Copyright © 1995 by Diane Berke

Printed in the United States of America

Library of Congress Cataloging-in-Publication Data

Berke, Diane.
    The gentle smile : practicing oneness in daily life / Diane Berke.
        p.   cm.
    Includes bibliographical references.
    ISBN 0-8245-1499-8
    1. Spiritual life. 2. Simplicity—Religious aspects. I. Title.
BL624.B463 1995
299'.93—dc20   95-11571
                                                                CIP

Lovingly dedicated

to the Spirit of Love and Wisdom
that lives within us all

to everyone who seeks to live
the way of a peaceful heart

and to Tony,
who helped me come back
to my smile

Contents

Acknowledgments

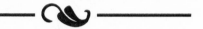

I am deeply grateful to so many who have contributed to the birthing of this book. Thank you from my heart to:

- The many teachers whose offerings of wisdom and love are cited here. Although most of them I know only through their writings, they have all gifted my life immeasurably.

- The members of Interfaith Fellowship and readers of *On Course* magazine, whose loving support, feedback, and encouragement are a continuing source of nourishment for me. A special thank-you to Jon Mundy, Jeff and Julie Olmsted, and Ruth Murphy for their love and friendship and for sharing their gifts and their love so generously.

- Michael Leach of the Crossroad Publishing Co. for his unfailing enthusiasm, encouragement, openness, and warmth.

- Michael Melia, my dear friend and colleague, who has taught me so much about self-acceptance and compassion. Thank you, Michael, for always seeing and supporting the best in me.

- The many wonderful friends with whom I share this life journey. Special thanks to Mark Tollefson, Pru Georgia, Michael Pergola, Tom and Linda Carpenter, Donna Cary, and Doug Lee.

- Elizabeth, Wally, and Winnie. Thank you for opening your hearts and welcoming me into the family. I feel very blessed to have you in my life.

- My sixteen-year-old cat, Rudy, who is an amazing teacher of forgiveness, equanimity, and boundless love.

- And, finally, Tony Zito, whose kindness, generosity, and loving support are reflected in every page of this book. Thank you for encouraging me to find my own voice, thank you for your enthusiasm and feedback, thank you for listening with an open heart, thank you for making me laugh, thank you for being here. I love you.

Credits

Grateful acknowledgment is made for permission to reprint excerpts from the following works:

From *A Course in Miracles.* © 1975, 1985, 1992 by The Foundation for Inner Peace, Mill Valley, Calif. Reprinted by permission of The Foundation for Inner Peace.

From *Coming to Life: Traveling the Spiritual Path in Everyday Life*, by Polly Berrien Berends. © 1990 by Polly Berrien Berends. Reprinted by permission of HarperCollins Publishers, Inc.

From *A Pocketful of Miracles,* by Joan Borysenko. © 1994 by Joan Borysenko. Reprinted by permission of Warner Books, Inc.

From *I Am with You Always,* by Douglas Bloch. © 1992 by Douglas Bloch. Reprinted by permission of Bantam Books, a division of Bantam Doubleday Dell Publishing Group, Inc.

From *Chicken Soup for the Soul,* written and compiled by Jack Canfield and Mark Victor Hansen. © 1993 by Jack Canfield and Mark Victor Hansen. Reprinted by permission of Health Communications, Inc.

From *The Dragon Doesn't Live Here Anymore,* by Alan Cohen. © 1981, 1990 by Alan Cohen. Reprinted by permission of Random House.

From *Pilgrim at Tinker Creek*, by Annie Dillard. © 1974 by Annie Dillard. Reprinted by permission of HarperCollins Publishers, Inc.

From *5 Minutes for World Peace...Forever,* by Ruth Fishel. © 1991 by Ruth Fishel. Reprinted by permission of Health Communications, Inc.

From *A Spirituality Named Compassion* by Matthew Fox. © 1979 by Matthew Fox. Reprinted by permission of HarperCollins Publishers, Inc.

From *Man's Search for Meaning,* by Viktor E. Frankl. © 1959, 1962, 1984 by Viktor Frankl. Reprinted by permission of Beacon Press.

From *Seeking the Heart of Wisdom,* by Joseph Goldstein and Jack Kornfield. © 1987 by Joseph Goldstein and Jack Kornfield. Reprinted by permission of Shambhala Publications.

From *Heart of the Koran,* by Lex Hixon. © 1988 by Lex Hixon. Reprinted by permission of Quest Books, The Theosophical Publishing House.

From *A Path with Heart,* by Jack Kornfield. © 1993 by Jack Kornfield. Reprinted by permission of Bantam Books, a division of Bantam Doubleday Dell Publishing Group, Inc.

From *Guided Meditations, Explorations, and Healings,* by Stephen Levine. © 1991 by Stephen Levine. Reprinted by permission of Doubleday, a division of Bantam Doubleday Dell Publishing Group, Inc.

From *Healing into Life and Death,* by Stephen Levine. © 1987 by Stephen Levine. Reprinted by permission of Doubleday, a division of Bantam Doubleday Dell Publishing Group, Inc.

From *Mary's Way,* by Peggy Tabor Millin. © 1991 by Peggy Tabor Millin. Reprinted by permission of Celestial Arts, Berkeley, Calif.

From *Peace Pilgrim: Her Life and Work in Her Own Words,* compiled by Friends of Peace Pilgrim. © 1982, 1988 by Friends of Peace Pilgrim. Reprinted by permission of Friends of Peace Pilgrim, Hemet, Calif.

From *How Can I Help?: Stories and Reflections on Service,* by Ram Dass and Paul Gorman. © 1985 by Ram Dass and Paul Gorman. Reprinted by permission of Alfred A. Knopf, Inc.

From *Bridges to Heaven: How Well-Known Seekers Define and Deepen Their Connection with God,* edited by Jonathan Robinson. © 1994 by Jonathan Robinson. Reprinted by permission of Stillpoint Publishing.

From *The Tibetan Book of Living and Dying,* by Sogyal Rinpoche. © 1993 by Rigpa Fellowship. Reprinted by permission of HarperCollins.

From *Being Peace,* by Thich Nhat Hanh. © 1987 by Thich Nhat Hanh. Reprinted by permission of Parallax Press, Berkeley, Calif.

From *Peace Is Every Step,* by Thich Nhat Hanh. © 1991 by Thich Nhat Hanh. Reprinted by permission of Bantam Books, a division of Bantam Doubleday Dell Publishing Group, Inc.

From *Present Moment, Wonderful Moment: Mindfulness Verses for Daily Living,* by Thich Nhat Hanh. © 1990 by Thich Nhat Hanh. Reprinted by permission of Parallax Press, Berkeley, Calif. Excerpt by Thich Nhat Hanh in *One*

Hundred Graces, edited by Marcia and Jack Kelly (Bell Tower, 1992) originally appeared in *Present Moment, Wonderful Moment: Mindfulness Verses for Daily Living,* by Thich Nhat Hanh (1990) and is reprinted by permission of Parallax Press, Berkeley, Calif.

From *The Miracle of Mindfulness: A Manual on Meditation,* by Thich Nhat Hanh. © 1975, 1976 by Thich Nhat Hanh. Reprinted by permission of Beacon Press.

From *To See Differently,* by Susan Trout. © 1990 by Susan Trout. Reprinted by permission of the author and Three Roses Press.

From *Finding Your Strength in Difficult Times,* by David Viscott. © 1993 by David Viscott. Reprinted by permission of Contemporary Books, Chicago.

From *Glossary-Index for A Course in Miracles,* by Kenneth Wapnick. © 1982, 1986, 1989, 1994 by the Foundation for "A Course in Miracles." Reprinted by permission of the author and the Foundation for "A Course in Miracles."

Efforts have been made to obtain all needed permissions for this book. If any required acknowledgments have been omitted, it is unintentional. If notified, the publishers will be pleased to rectify any omission in future editions.

Referencing Key
for Quotations from
A Course in Miracles

Note: All quotations from *A Course in Miracles* contained in this book are reprinted by permission of The Foundation for Inner Peace, P.O. Box 598, Mill Valley, CA 94942. The ideas and viewpoint presented here reflect the understanding, interpretation, and experience of the author and do not necessarily express the views of those who hold the copyright on the Course.

Passages quoted from *A Course in Miracles* are referenced in the following standard way:

> T: Text
> W: Workbook
> M: Manual for Teachers
> C: Clarification of Terms

Each passage cited contains two references. The first refers to the first edition of the Course, published in 1976. The second refers to the second edition, published in 1992.

Examples:

— T. p. 200; T-12.I.3:1–4

T. p. 200 — Text (1st edition), page 200

T-12 — Text (2d edition), Chapter 12

I — Subsection I of the chapter

3 — Paragraph 3 of the subsection

1–4 — Sentences 1 through 4 of the paragraph

— W. p. 218; W-Pt.I.124.4

W. p. 218 — Workbook (1st edition), page 218

W-Pt.I. — Workbook (2d edition), Part I

124 — Lesson 124

4 — Paragraph 4 of the lesson

— M. p. 3; M-1.4:2

M. p. 3 — Manual for Teachers (1st edition), page 3

M-1 — Manual for Teachers (2d edition), Question 1

4 — Paragraph 4 of Question 1

2 — Sentence 2 of Paragraph 4

— M. p. 77; C-2.6:2–13

M. p. 77 — Manual for Teachers (1st edition), page 77

C-2 — Clarification of Terms (2d edition), Section 2 (Note: The Clarification of Terms is the last part of the Manual for Teachers)

6 — Paragraph 6 of Section 2

2–13 — Sentences 2 through 13 of Paragraph 6

Preface

I do not think of myself as an individual but rather as an embodiment of the heart of the world which is pleading for peace.... My mission is to help promote peace by helping others to find inner *peace. If I can find it, you can find it too. Peace is an idea whose time has come.*

— PEACE PILGRIM, *Her Life and Work in Her Own Words*

At a recent workshop I presented in Atlanta, I asked participants to share why they had chosen to attend this particular workshop. One man answered that he wanted to see with his own eyes whether and how someone could actually live in New York City and still manage to be peaceful.

I live in New York City — the one place that, as I was growing up in Lancaster, Pennsylvania, I swore I would never live. Life, it turned out, had a sense of humor about my "vow," and I have lived in New York now for nearly twenty years. Some days I am very peaceful here. Some days I am not. But I have learned without a doubt that my experience of peace has far less to do with my surroundings than with the state of my own mind and heart.

Whether we live in New York City or anywhere else, inner peace is perhaps our deepest — and most elusive — human longing. Peace is certainly the great need of a world and a time in which chaos, uncertainty, conflict, and violence are escalating. So many of the ways and places we've sought — and perhaps, for a time, believed we found — happiness, security, and meaning in life have failed us, leaving us empty, disappointed, fearful.

Historically and culturally we have tried nearly everything to create peace around us. We have legislated peace, marched for peace, made bargains for peace, threatened and manipulated for peace, even fought and died for peace. Our efforts have failed. Such efforts will always fail.

Our efforts have failed because we have, for the most part, not yet learned to *live* in peace. We have not learned to live peacefully within ourselves, with our families, co-workers, and neighbors. Teachers in every spiritual tradition have told us that there can be no peace in the world until there is peace in our hearts. We have heard their teaching, but most of us have yet to put it sincerely into practice in our lives.

> *The key word for our time is* practice.
> *We have all the light we need,*
> *we just need to put it into practice.*
>
> — Peace Pilgrim, *Her Life and Work*
> *in Her Own Words*

G. K. Chesterton once wrote, "It is not that Christianity has been tried and found wanting. Rather it has been found difficult and left untried." The same could be said of the teachings of peace and universal love that form the heart of every spiritual and religious tradition.

Yet we are also living in a time of perhaps unprecedented possibility, as more and more people are turning to spiritual perspective to find meaning and direction for their own lives. Perhaps we are moving, individually and collectively, toward the maturity and humility needed to do the consistent and practical inner work required to cultivate a peaceful heart. This inner work asks of us a sincere dedication, honesty, and patience with ourselves. Yet at this moment in history, and in our individual lives, there is no work more essential for us to do.

Some years ago, I heard a minister give a sermon in which he suggested that the traditional Christmas blessing — "Peace on earth, good will to all" — was, in fact, backward. *First,* he said, we need to cultivate good will toward all. First we need to recognize our fundamental kinship — our brotherhood and sisterhood — with all creation. From that awareness and recognition, we need to let a spirit of compassion and loving kindness toward all that lives be born and take root in our hearts. With attentive nurturing and care, from that seed can grow a boundless and abiding love, a universal love, a love that naturally dissolves conflict and quiets fear. In the presence of that love, there can be only peace. If we truly cultivate and nurture good will in our hearts toward everyone, peace on earth must one day follow.

My spiritual path and practice for many years has been *A Course in Miracles.* The goal of the Course is inner peace, and its primary practice is forgiveness. Forgiveness in the framework of the Course is a process of letting go of condemnation and blame, reclaiming the images of guilt and unworthiness we have projected onto the world, and shifting in our minds from fearful to loving perceptions of others and ourselves. Through forgiveness our identification with the ego is gradually loosened and dissolved, and we are restored to the peace that is our fundamental nature as spirit.

Although the Course is my primary spiritual practice, my basic spiritual orientation since childhood has been strongly interfaith. I have always sought and been drawn to what seems to be universal in spiritual teaching and understanding. In addition to the Course and my Western Judeo-Christian heritage, I feel a deep and profound resonance and appreciation for the teachings of Buddhism, especially as I have encountered them in the writings of Thich Nhat Hanh, Stephen Levine, Jack Kornfield, and Sogyal Rinpoche.

The Gentle Smile is an attempt to bring together my exploration of these teachings with my understanding of the Course, transpersonal psychology, and perennial spiritual wisdom. I regret any distortion to the wisdom and beauty of any of these teachings that may result from the limitations of my own experience or understanding of them.

As a writer, I write primarily, not about what I have mastered, but about what I need to deepen and practice. *The Gentle Smile* is about my own search for inner peace, through trying to understand and cultivate the qualities of loving kindness, compassion, joy in the success and happiness of others, nonattachment, and equanimity. It is my deep wish and sincere hope that it will be helpful to others who seek peace in their hearts and lives.

> *May peace extend from our hearts and minds*
> *to bless the world with peace.*

DIANE BERKE

New York City
Christmas 1994

Chapter 1

Living Wisely, Loving Well

The personal life, deeply lived,
always expands into truths beyond itself.

— ANAÏS NIN

Earth's the right place for love:
I don't know where it's likely to go better.

— ROBERT FROST

Insight meditation teacher Jack Kornfield has pointed out that when we reach the end of our lives, we are left with only a few simple questions: Did I learn to live wisely? Did I love well? These two questions address the very essence of our human experience. To those of us on the spiritual journey, they speak to the fruits of all our efforts and practice.

A paradox of the spiritual journey is that we come to know our deeper reality as spirit through the process of understanding and accepting ourselves as human beings. Our humanity, explored and lived in a full and open-hearted way, is the gateway to awareness and experience of our divinity. Human life, with its impermanence and change, is the place that we can rediscover the eternal, changeless reality of what we are.

Although a number of spiritual paths teach that this world is a dream, illusion, *maya* (which means, literally, "what is not"), still this is where we find ourselves. This is where we believe that we are. This is our subjective, psychological reality. And so it is here, in the experience of this world, that we must begin to relearn the truth of our deeper, spiritual nature. It is through this human experience that we journey toward awakening.

Being human is the classroom in which we learn our lessons of spiritual growth and healing. The underlying core and purpose of all our learning is the undoing of everything that seems to separate us — from each other; from our Source; from knowing and experiencing our wholeness; from the joy, aliveness, and peace where we are most truly at home; from the flow and sharing of the love that is in our hearts. It is within and through our human experience that we come to be restored to "the awareness of love's presence" (*A Course in Miracles*, T-Intro.1:7). And it is this restoration that opens the way for our full awakening.

We cannot prepare our minds to awaken by disparaging the classroom or trying to avoid it. Our learning must be here, in living our lives as human beings. It is here that we learn to love. It is here that we learn to live wisely. It is here that we find our way home again to peace, to happiness, to God.

To say yes to the journey home is to embrace the experience of being human and let our daily lives become our spiritual practice. As we explore the depths and the heights of our being — opening to the simple yet profound workings of love within the human experience, learning to accept with compassion and understanding all of what we are and all of what life brings us — we discover God as a living presence in our human spirit and heart.

> *Out of the womb of the human heart,*
> *God is born.*
>
> — Sufi *Zikr* (Chant of Remembrance),
>   taught by Atum O'Kane

Separation — The Root Cause of Suffering

The spiritual journey is a journey of healing, a journey from pain and suffering to peace. This is healing at the very deepest levels of our being. The purpose of the journey is that we come to be liberated from our suffering by understanding and undoing its cause.

In Buddhist teachings, the cause of all our suffering is *attachment,* which expresses itself in the polarities of desire and aversion. Attachment itself derives from ignorance of our true nature, from mistakenly identifying ourselves with the illusion of a separate self. Cherishing and grasping for the preservation and pleasure of this self, we often find that we are out of harmony with others, with the realities of human life, with the deeper demands of our own life and growth process. The experience of separation leads inevitably to a permeating quality of conflict and fear in our lives.

This sense of, or belief in, a separated self is referred to in spiritual teaching as the *ego.* Identification with the ego is the very root of all our suffering. Jack Kornfield writes,

Whenever we think of ourselves as separate, fear and attachment arise and we grow constricted, defensive, ambitious and territorial. To protect the separate self, we push certain things away, while to bolster it we hold onto other things and identify with them.

— JACK KORNFIELD, *A Path with Heart*

A Course in Miracles also teaches that the source of our suffering is our belief in separation and identification with the ego. In the language of the Course, this is the belief that we have separated ourselves from God and from our Self, which is the extension of God.

The problem, according to the Course, is not the thought of separation in and of itself. The problem is that we have taken this thought *seriously,* invested it with the power of our belief and identification. When that occurred, the Course teaches, it is as if we had fallen asleep to reality and begun dreaming a dream of separation. It is this dream that we now experience as the reality of our existence.

The basic thought of separation occurs in our minds in many expressions and disguises. It is manifested as guilt, fear, unworthiness, inadequacy, and their defensive opposites, specialness, superiority, grandiosity. We construct concepts around these images and identify those concepts as "self." We then do everything we can to cling to, defend, and preserve this self. In this way we continue to take the idea of separation seriously, and we remain in our dream state.

Guilt and Projection

In Judeo-Christian terminology, the birth of the ego is described in the story of Adam and Eve's fall from grace, the experience of expulsion from the Garden of Eden. The thought of separation, in this framework, is a thought of sin and guilt. The Course points out that to believe that we have separated from God is to believe that we have *attacked* God, that we have somehow shattered the perfect unity and peace of Heaven. While this may not be a consciously held belief, the existential guilt and nameless anxiety that haunt the dark, fearful places of our human psyche point to its presence in our minds.

The profound guilt that arises from the belief that we have separated from God is psychologically intolerable to us. We defend against experiencing this guilt — and the inevitable fear and expectation of punishment it generates — first by repressing (denying) it, and then by projecting it out. We see the origin of separation, attack, guilt, and fear as being outside of ourselves rather than in the workings of our own minds. We displace, rather than undo, the source of our experience of separation and guilt.

We become caught up in ever-deepening cycles of attack, defense, and counterattack. Peace of mind and heart, an abiding sense of security, happiness, and well-being seem hopelessly alien to us, impossible and unrealistic longings in an uncertain, hostile, and dangerous world. How can we find our way out of such a nightmarish existence?

Healing Our Suffering — Undoing the Belief in Separation

Both Buddhism and the Course teach that separation is not reality, but illusion. Albert Einstein described it as an "optical delusion" of our consciousness. Still, we have traveled deep into this delusion and become lost in it.

It has been said that getting lost in the illusion of separation is, in a sense, the first step on the journey of awakening. Becoming *aware* that we are lost propels us to seek a path that will lead us home. Becoming truthful about our suffering — and about the repeated failure of our worldly attempts to escape from it — we begin to seek a deeper understanding of where it comes from and how to free ourselves of it.

> *Tolerance for pain may be high, but it is not without limit. Eventually everyone begins to recognize, however dimly, that there* must *be a better way.*
>
> —T. p. 18; T-2.III.3:5–6

If the source of suffering fundamentally rests in our belief in the illusion of separation, then release from suffering comes with undoing our experience of separation. We are healed and set free as the *reality of oneness* dawns again in our awareness.

> *Only awareness of our oneness with the whole can heal us from the nightmare of separateness and the fear, pain, and frustration arising from it. Only awareness of our oneness with a guiding force beyond the self can free us from the anxiety of trying to be on our own and the hurt of relying*

overmuch on others. This alone can make us truly intelligent, peaceful, well, loving, spontaneous, and free.

— POLLY BERRIEN BERENDS, *Coming to Life*

To rediscover our oneness with the whole of life, we need to uncover the source of our experience of separation. We need to be willing to go back into our minds, to witness and understand how separation is born and sustained in our thinking and perception.

Rarely do we look closely enough to recognize the source of our suffering within our own thoughts. But this is where liberation and healing begin. What the Course calls a "miracle" is the inner shift by which we reclaim our power as the source of our own perception and experience. Recognizing that the source of our suffering and unhappiness is within, in our own minds, we begin to recognize that the answer, the source of peace, lies within us as well.

As we go back into our minds, we find that there are two very different voices within us. One is the voice of the ego, the voice of separation and fear. The other is the voice of spirit, the voice of clarity, wisdom, and love. This voice, this presence of truth in our minds, is our true source of peace. The Course calls this presence the Holy Spirit, the Voice for God. Tibetan Buddhist teacher Sogyal Rinpoche calls it the "hidden spiritual being," the "wise guide," or our *discriminating awareness*.

Two people have been living in you all your life. One is the ego, garrulous, demanding, hysterical, calculating; the other is the hidden spiritual being, whose still voice of wisdom you have only rarely heard or attended to.

— SOGYAL RINPOCHE, *The Tibetan Book of Living and Dying*

As we journey on our spiritual path, as we listen to and work with the teachings of spiritual truth and integrate them into our living, we become increasingly able to differentiate the "various clamoring and enthralling voices of ego" from this still voice of wisdom and guidance. As this occurs, the memory of our real nature, "with all its splendor and confidence" starts to return to us.

As we gradually begin to disidentify from the ego, we discover that it is not the truth of who and what we are.

> *You will find, in fact, that you have uncovered in yourself your own wise guide.... The more often you listen to this wise guide, the more easily you will be able to change your negative moods ... see through them, and even laugh at the absurd dramas and ridiculous illusions that they are.... If you follow the voice of your wise guide, the voice of your discriminating awareness, and let the ego fall silent, you come to experience that presence of wisdom and joy and bliss that you really are.*
>
> — SOGYAL RINPOCHE, *The Tibetan Book of Living and Dying*

The Course also teaches that as we listen to the voice of the Holy Spirit, we find that we can learn to laugh gently at the ego's dramas and foolish games. As we learn to see through them, in a sense they disappear. And where they seemed to be we find again our true Self, the Christ in us, the perfect and radiant Self that God created.

We can use the terms "wise guide" or "Holy Spirit" interchangeably. This voice is not something foreign or outside us. But it *is* outside — that is, *beyond* — our ego. It is the deeper wisdom of our own mind that knows its perfect unity with Divine Mind. It is in joining with this deeper wisdom, in shifting our identification from the ego self to the greater Self, that we come to true healing.

Going Back into Our Minds

> *To become the spectator of one's own life*
> *is to escape the suffering of life.*
>
> — OSCAR WILDE

The healing process offered by the Course is one of "bringing the darkness to the light," so that the darkness of the ego in our

minds can be gently and naturally dispelled by the light of awareness and truth. Course teacher Ken Wapnick describes this as the
process of looking at our fearful ego thoughts — thoughts of separation, specialness, attack, punishment, loss, anger, hatred, and
vengeance — with the love of the Holy Spirit beside us.

We need not, the Course tells us, go searching for love or truth.
Rather we need to bring to light the barriers in our minds, in
our thinking, that keep us unaware of the love and truth already
within us. As we look at our ego thoughts and beliefs with the
Holy Spirit, we begin to learn that they are not real and have no
power to hurt us. As we let them go, and with them our fear,
the light that has always been in our minds is restored to our
awareness.

Similarly, Buddhist meditation teacher Stephen Levine writes,

*Our work is not so much to open the heart — which like the
sun is always shining, but whose light is often obscured —
but to open the mind so that the deep light of the essence of
mind we call the heart can shine through.*

— STEPHEN LEVINE, *Guided Meditations, Explorations, and Healings*

This understanding of the heart — as a deep essence of mind
whose light is always shining but is obscured by our closed-
minded, fearful thinking — is similar to what has been called the
light of Christ within our minds. What Levine describes as "the
hindrances to the heart — the self-interest, the fear, the separatism,
the judgment," are what the Course would call "the blocks to the
awareness of love's presence" (T-Intro.1:7) These hindrances or
blocks are simply the varied manifestations of the ego, the belief
in a separated self.

It is possible to look at the ego from *within* the ego thought system, that is, to judge, condemn, be fearful of, and hateful toward
the ego. It is also possible to look at the ego from *outside* the ego
thought system, to look with simple awareness and recognition.

It is as we look at the ego from outside the ego — without judgment or fear, with only acceptance and mercy and love — that it

begins to dawn on us that the ego cannot be who we are. This is what the Course refers to as joining with the Holy Spirit and practicing forgiveness. Stephen Levine describes it as bringing the mind into the heart, letting the contents of mind "float" in the spacious awareness of the heart.

When we are lost in our identification with the ego we live in deep suffering and fear. As we loosen the bonds of that identification in our minds, we are released to the joy and freedom that are our birthright as spirit. We can be lost in the ego, or we can witness the ego with love. One is enslavement, the other release.

The difference between receiving thought in a merciful awareness and being lost in thinking is the difference between liberation and bondage.

— STEPHEN LEVINE, *Guided Meditations, Explorations, and Healings*

This ability to witness the ego with love, to "receive thought in merciful awareness," is developed through the practice of *mindfulness*.

Mindfulness

Just remain in the center watching,
and then forget you are there.

— LAO TZU

To be mindful is to be present in
your higher self
rather than your ego.

— JOAN BORYSENKO

There is a teaching in the *Tao Te Ching* that "muddy water, let stand, will clear." The process of healing is the process of learning to look at the ego — at our ego thoughts and the feelings these

thoughts generate — and *doing nothing*. One of the common pit-
falls for students of the Course and other spiritual paths is the
temptation to judge, resist, fight against, suppress, deny, or try to
get rid of our ego thoughts and feelings. But anything we try to
do about the ego keeps stirring up and muddying the water. Anything we try to do about the ego simply reinforces our belief in its
reality and binds us further to illusion.

The alternative is to step back in our minds and look at the ego
and its manifestations in our thoughts, feelings, and actions without judgment or upset. If we can look at the ego from outside the
ego — that is, without judgment, guilt, and fear — then the ego
cannot be who we really are. When we can look at the ego and
gently smile, we begin to recover ourselves and the peace and basic
happiness inherent in our true connectedness with all life.

> *The holy instant is a gentle smile.*
>
> — KEN WAPNICK,
> IN "THE HOLY INSTANT,"
> ROSCOE, N.Y., MARCH 1991

The Course calls this practicing the holy instant, joining with
the Holy Spirit, seeing with the Vision of Christ. Buddhist teaching calls it the practice of mindfulness. The state of mindfulness
has sometimes been described as sitting on the bank of a river
and simply watching the river flow by. As you watch, all kinds
of things may float past you in the water — fallen leaves and
branches, empty beer cans and old tires, mysterious containers
and intriguing packages. The river represents the flow and movement of consciousness or mind. What floats by in the river are the
specific contents of consciousness — thoughts, feelings, sensations,
memories, fantasies, and so on.

In our typical ego-bound state, we let ourselves be "caught" by
what floats by. We jump into the river, grab on to something, and
let it carry us downstream. In a mindful state, we simply sit on the
river bank and watch it all flow past, our peace undisturbed. We

do not have to identify with anything that floats past us. We can understand that none of it is what we truly are.

Mindfulness is a purposeful, accepting, nonjudging state of mind that allows us to observe the workings of the conditioned or ego-mind and to open into the deeper reality of our true being. In transpersonal psychology, mindfulness is described as the *witness* state of consciousness. In the Course it is called "right-mindedness."

In a mindful, or right-minded, state we remember to *look without judgment*. We see with the clear-sighted vision of acceptance and love. The practice of mindfulness cultivates wisdom. We begin to see clearly into the workings of the mind and all that it gives rise to in our experience. Through mindful witness, we develop the ability to see the empty, illusory nature of the ego and its world by recognizing its origins within our own mental processes.

Mindfulness moves us into deeper understanding, appreciation, and love for others and ourselves — ultimately for everyone and everything. This in turn helps us awaken to the changeless reality behind all appearances of impermanence and separation.

Life as Meditation

Mindfulness can be cultivated through the practice of formal meditation. Clear instruction for beginning mindfulness meditation practice can be found in the writings of Jack Kornfield and Joseph Goldstein, Stephen Levine, Thich Nhat Hanh, and Sogyal Rinpoche. The Workbook lessons in the Course also provide a structure for developing mindfulness, or learning to share the perception of the Holy Spirit. The fuller practice of mindfulness, however, or of any spiritual practice, is intended to reach beyond formal practice into the dailyness of our lives.

To be mindful is to be aware, open, and present to each moment. We can practice mindfulness in such a way that life itself becomes our meditation. Thich Nhat Hanh, a Vietnamese Buddhist monk and teacher, suggests that we can use *gathas,* mindfulness verses, in connection with mundane activities to help us remember our deeper purpose as we go through our day.

One of my favorite gathas is one he suggests we use as we begin to eat a meal.

> *With the first taste,*
> *I promise to practice loving kindness.*
> *With the second,*
> *I promise to relieve the suffering of others.*
> *With the third,*
> *I promise to see others' joy as my own.*
> *With the fourth,*
> *I promise to learn the way of nonattachment*
> *and equanimity.*
>
> — THICH NHAT HANH, QUOTED IN
> *One Hundred Graces,*
> ED. MARCIA AND JACK KELLY

When I first read this verse, I immediately felt my heart open. I experienced both a spaciousness and fullness of heart, a deep and expansive feeling of love for all beings. In Buddhist teaching, love and wisdom are described as the "two wings of the Dharma" (Joseph Goldstein, *Insight Meditation*). Both are considered essential to enlightenment. Each enriches and expands our potential for the other.

Love both arises from and deepens our realization of our oneness with all that lives. With love in our hearts, we can look upon everyone we meet as a friend and all creation as our family. We can experience in a living way the beautiful teaching that "there are no strangers in God's creation" (T. p. 37; T-3.III.7:7).

Practicing Oneness

The mindfulness verse for beginning to eat is based on what is referred to in Buddhism as the "four immeasurable states," or the "heavenly abodes." These are the qualities or practices of loving kindness (*metta*), compassion (*karuna*), sympathetic joy (*mudita*), and nonattachment and equanimity (*upekkha*).

As I reflected on these four promises, they seemed to me to offer a helpful and practical framework for translating the concept of oneness — the idea that we are one with all creation — into everyday living. They gave me a concrete way to think about the *practice of oneness* in daily life.

The rest of this book will explore these four promises. Each chapter that discusses one of these is followed by a chapter that explores a related quality or practice that can serve to deepen the practice of that promise. Self-acceptance helps deepen our ability to practice loving kindness. Service is a way to express and further cultivate the quality of compassion in our lives. Practicing appreciation and gratitude makes it easier for us to develop our capacity to rejoice in the happiness of others. Exercising our power to choose blessing in the face of adversity deepens our stance of nonattachment and equanimity.

The capacity to love fully, to live wisely, to awaken from the nightmare of separation into the joy of our true nature is within each one of us. It exists as a seed, a potential within us. As we cultivate that potential in ourselves, we help others do the same.

> *In each woman, in each man, there is a capacity of waking up, of understanding, and of loving. . . . Some people allow it to develop, and some do not, but everyone has it. This capacity of waking up . . . is called the Buddha nature. . . . Since the baby of that Buddha is in us, we should give him or her a chance.*
>
> — THICH NHAT HANH, *Being Peace*

My prayer is that this book may, in some small way, help us give the "baby" of our Buddha-nature — the seed of God within us — a chance to grow and mature and live in joyful expression in our human lives.

Chapter 2

Loving Kindness

I promise to practice loving kindness.

Three things in human life are important:
The first is to be kind. The second is to be kind.
And the third is to be kind.

— HENRY JAMES

In the beginning we attempt
to cultivate loving kindness.
Later, loving kindness cultivates us.

— STEPHEN LEVINE

As he reached the end of his life, philosopher Aldous Huxley concluded a lifetime's work and thought in this way:

It's a bit embarrassing to have been concerned with the human problem all one's life and find at the end that one has no more to offer by way of advice than "try to be a little kinder."

Loving kindness forms the heart of the teachings of all the world's religions. The Talmud summarizes the whole of Jewish moral teaching in this way: "Kindness is the beginning and the end of the law." Jesus said that we are his true disciples only as we love one another. The Koran teaches, "The deep human response for which Allah Most Merciful calls is the commitment to justice that transforms daily life into continual acts of kindness and generosity toward all persons, regarding them as one intimate family" (16:89, rendered by Lex Hixon, in *Heart of the Koran*). Paramahansa Yogananda implores us to "be...a cosmic friend, imbued with kindness and affection for all God's creation, scattering love everywhere." And the Dalai Lama states, "My religion is simple. My religion is kindness."

Loving kindness refers, at its core, to a simple, basic care and wish for the shared happiness, peace, and well-being of all living beings. It is a wish for healing, for release from all forms of suffering and fear, for freedom and wholeness and the gladness that comes from dwelling in the open heart. We can offer and extend loving kindness both to others and to ourselves.

A subscriber to our magazine, *On Course,* recently sent me a story, reprinted from an ecumenical newsletter, that beautifully conveys the gentle spirit of loving kindness.

A few years ago at the Seattle Special Olympics, nine contestants, all physically or mentally disabled, assembled at the starting line for the 100-yard dash. At the gun, they all started out, not exactly in a dash, but with a relish to run the race to the finish and win. All, that is, except one boy who stumbled on the asphalt, tumbled over a couple of times and began to cry. The other eight heard the boy cry. They slowed down and looked back. Then they all turned around and went back. Every one of them. One girl with Down's syndrome bent down and kissed him and said, "This will make it better." Then all nine linked arms and walked together to the finish line.

— From *EcuMemo,* September/October 1994

The story went on to describe that the crowd in the stadium stood and cheered for several minutes, everyone deeply affected by what they had witnessed. As we forget the self-cherishing concerns of our ego, the simple, natural goodness in our hearts reaches out to relieve the suffering of others and to share in success and celebration with them.

We are touched deeply by witnessing or hearing about acts of selfless kindness and love because such expressions reconnect us with a deeper possibility and truth in ourselves. The times that we live from and give expression to the simple goodness and caring of our hearts are, in the end, what give true meaning and value to our lives.

Jack Kornfield suggests a meditation in which we imagine that we are at the end of our lives, some time in the future. From that vantage point we look back over our lives and let two good deeds, two things we've done that were good, come to mind. Once we've let these memories arise, we reflect carefully on the quality of these situations, "at what is comprised in a moment of goodness picked out of a lifetime of words and actions."

Almost inevitably, he points out, the kinds of things that come to people's mind are very simple — simple gestures and expressions of human kindness and love.

The things that matter most in our lives are not fantastic or grand. They are the moments when we touch one another, when we are there in the most attentive or caring way. This simple and profound intimacy is the love that we all long for.

— JACK KORNFIELD, *A Path with Heart*

Loving kindness carries with it enormous power to transform and heal. For it teaches us, simply and directly, that we are not alone. Loving kindness soothes the pain of separation in our hearts with a balm of sweetness, as this lovely Christmas story shows:

Our church was celebrating Christmas Eve with a children's program. Its chapel had special memories for me. Only eight months previously, the memorial service for my husband of forty-four years had been held there.

On my own now, I settled into a seat near the aisle. During the opening prayer I noticed a young girl about ten years old, standing in the aisle looking for a place to sit. Motioning her to come in, I turned my knees, and the girl slid past and sat down.

The beautiful program continued with the children participating in songs, poems and recitals. The climax was the singing of "Silent Night." As the children's voices chorused this most beautiful of Christmas hymns, memories of past Christmases with my husband flooded back. My eyes filled with tears and I held a handkerchief to my mouth, trying to control myself. Then I felt my neighbor's small hand creep into my lap. She took my hand and gave it a comforting squeeze. My heart swelled with sudden joy.

As I look back on that evening, I give thanks for this simplest and loveliest of Christmas gifts — the touch of a hand.

— *Reader's Digest*, DECEMBER 1982

The Basis for Loving Kindness

There is a beautiful Hindu teaching, "To those in whom love dwells, all the world is one family." Loving kindness is the natural expression of recognizing our kinship with all creation.

The practice of loving kindness is based on a deep acknowledgment both of our God-given worth — our fundamental worthiness to be loved — and of the deprivation and terrible pain we have caused ourselves by forgetting that worth, by believing in the separation and thus depriving ourselves of love. Loving kindness is the wish to offer healing and restoration to all who are both "so deprived and so deserving of love" (Stephen Levine) — which is all of us, the whole of the separated and fragmented Sonship of creation.

We all suffer the terror and pain of the ego, the belief in separation, no matter how different its manifestations in our experience seem to be. And we all share the need for the one response that heals our pain and brings us peace: love. The Dalai Lama repeatedly stresses in his teachings that we need to remember that all beings want to be happy and to escape suffering. We want that and everyone else wants that too. We share that common goal and purpose. The Course points out that what shares a common purpose must be the same, must be one.

The promise to practice loving kindness is an acknowledgment of this oneness, of the commonality of purpose we share. From this awareness, there can be no real grounds for conflict — no grounds for anything to interfere with the natural expression of loving kindness and good will toward everyone and every living thing. We understand that what blesses any part of us blesses all. And so we dedicate ourselves to developing this awareness by practicing directing loving kindness toward ourselves, toward another, toward all.

> *Spread love everywhere you go.... Let no one ever come to you without leaving better and happier. Be the living expression of God's kindness: kindness in your face, kindness in your eyes, kindness in your smile, kindness in your warm greeting.*
>
> — MOTHER TERESA

Loving Kindness Meditation — *Metta*

While loving kindness is a natural response when our hearts are soft and open, a basic attitude of loving kindness is also something that we can cultivate and develop. In Buddhist teaching this is accomplished through the meditation practice known as *metta*.

Metta meditation is sometimes described as a process of "gentling the heart." It is based on the teaching of the Buddha that

> *Hatred is never overcome by hatred.*
> *Hatred is overcome only by love.*
> *That is the unalterable law.*
>
> — FROM *The Dhammapada*

Metta meditation gradually deepens and expands our capacity and ability to direct feelings and blessings of loving kindness toward ourselves, family and friends, colleagues, acquaintances, strangers, those we've seen as enemies, and all living beings everywhere.

In metta practice, we begin by allowing a feeling of love to converge in our hearts. Sogyal Rinpoche suggests that we can do this by remembering a time when someone treated us with kindness and love, and allowing that feeling of being loved to come alive in us again.

Those who have difficulty finding such a memory with another person might have felt that unconditional love from an animal, a pet. Or they might imagine receiving the love of a spiritual figure, such as Jesus or Mary or Buddha. We can also remember or imagine receiving kindness and love through nature: through the shining warmth of the sun or the tender caress of a soft breeze on our skin; through the sheltering shade of a maple tree, or the supporting firmness of the earth as we lie on our backs in a meadow; through the explosion of fragrance and color of a field of wildflowers. Joan Borysenko suggests imagining a wash of light pouring over us and feeling ourselves bathed in love, surrounded and held within an egg of light.

The *source* of our feeling loved is not important. But the *feeling of being loved* is extremely helpful. The love we feel in our own hearts overflows to bring the blessings of loving kindness to this world. As we are taught in the New Testament, we love because first we were loved.

We begin by directing this love toward ourselves, by offering ourselves wishes for our happiness, peace, and freedom from suffering and fear. Jack Kornfield points out that we begin with ourselves because without loving ourselves it is nearly impossible to love others.

After sending loving kindness to ourselves, we begin to extend it to others, addressing them directly in our minds and hearts. We begin with someone close to us, someone for whom we already have feelings of warmth and caring. As our capacity to love deepens and increases, we expand this part of our practice to include others. Eventually we find that we can send metta even to the difficult people in our lives, even to the people with whom we have experienced conflict and pain.

Finally, we conclude metta practice by offering blessings of loving kindness to the whole world, to all beings, everywhere.

Among my favorite of the blessings to use for metta practice are those offered by Stephen Levine in his book *Healing into Life and Death:*

> *May I (you, all beings) dwell in the heart.*
> *May I (you, all beings) be free of suffering.*
> *May I (you, all beings) be healed.*
> *May I (you, all beings) be at peace.*

Joan Borysenko suggests these beautiful expressions of metta in her book of daily practices, *Pocketful of Miracles:*

> *May I (you) be at peace, May my (your) heart remain open,*
> *May I (you) awaken to the light of my (your) own true nature,*
> *May I (you) be healed, May I (you) be a source of healing for all beings.*
>
> *May there be peace on earth, May the hearts of all people be open to themselves and each other,*
> *May all people awaken to the light of their true nature,*
> *May all creation be blessed and be a blessing to All That Is.*

The particular phrases we use in metta are less important than that our words carry a sincere message of kindness and love, a heart-felt wish for the happiness, freedom, well-being, and peace of others and ourselves.

There is a teaching in the Quaker tradition that "the service begins when the meeting is over." While formal metta meditation is spiritual service in and of itself, our aspiration is that the whole of our lives become the place of our metta practice. We seek to bring this basic attitude of loving kindness to each moment of our lives and to every interaction we have with everyone.

Joining First with Love

It is important to reiterate that practicing loving kindness meditation is not simply a matter of saying certain words or visualizing sending light to someone. To be an instrument of love in any way, we must ourselves be centered in the heart, joined with the love within us. Love naturally extends, for that is its nature. But to let love extend from us, we must be willing to witness and release in ourselves anything that blocks our own joining with love within, anything that keeps us out of our heart.

Stephen Levine describes this process in his own learning and practice:

> *When I first began doing this practice, if I found myself in disagreement with someone, I would begin to send loving kindness not so much to them, as at them. I thought I would "cool them out," thinking "what a good meditator I am." But I was angry. It was really my own suffering I needed to confront. I was the one who needed the loving kindness. And in time, I learned that I had to generate love for myself first before I could open to another. To send loving kindness at another with whom I was angry was an ancient superiority trip which just created more separation.*
>
> — STEPHEN LEVINE, *Guided Meditations, Explorations, and Healings*

He goes on to describe that as he was able to make room in his heart for himself, he developed the ability to relate to his own anger and frustration with the spaciousness and mercy that allowed it to dissolve. From there he could authentically relate in loving kindness to another. He concludes, "To send love to another we must first be in our heart."

This is analogous, in the framework of the Course, to realizing that we can never truly forgive anyone with our ego. The ego will sometimes appear to go through the motions of "forgiveness" in order to strengthen separation and difference (for example, to establish moral superiority and inferiority). But that is not true forgiveness.

When we find ourselves doing that, we need to be willing to forgive ourselves by looking at our own ego from the place of love in our hearts and minds. Joining with that love, we forgive the ego in ourselves and our brother and sister together. True forgiveness is an expression of true loving kindness.

Patience and Acceptance —
Loving Ourselves on the Way

> *Blessings on your journey,*
> *Blessings on your way,*
> *On your way back home...*
>
> — JOHN ASTIN, "CARRY THE LIGHT,"
> FROM *The Winds of Grace*

Our healing, our journey toward awakening, is a *process*. There is a saying that love brings up everything unlike itself to be purified and released. When we begin to practice loving kindness, and with each step we take in the direction of love we may find that all that is unloving in ourselves surfaces in our awareness and screams for our attention.

Without the proper context for understanding this, we can become easily discouraged and down on ourselves. The ego by nature is merciless in its judgment, and one of its common targets is our seeming lack of progress on the spiritual path. With our ego-mind, we attack ourselves for having an ego, for being fearful, for having our hearts closed, for not being loving enough.

But to practice loving kindness means to touch what is unloving within us with love instead of judgment, to deepen in our ability to meet our fear in all its forms with forgiveness, acceptance, kindness, and love.

> *Many have said that they would like to be more loving. They complain that, if they are to be "completely honest," their hearts aren't open more than a few moments a day — and that is a good day already!*
>
> *We are so merciless with ourselves. Any amount of love in this life of forgetfulness and violence is a miracle. Any amount of love in this world so calling for healing and peace is true grace. A few moments of peace, of lovingkindness, is a triumph over fear and old limitations.*
>
> — STEPHEN LEVINE, *Guided Meditations, Explorations, and Healings*

The Course reminds us that the Holy Spirit looks with love on all that He perceives — which means that He looks with love on us (T. p. 163; T-9.VII.3:1). There are no qualifications or conditions to this statement. There is a place within us where we do hold ourselves in perfect love, where we offer ourselves, not blame and judgment, but only mercy and healing.

Jesus reminds us in the Course that although he knows that fear is not real, we do not yet know that (T. p. 27; T-2.VII.1:3). That is what we are here to learn. And so we need to honor and be patient with the process by which we bring our fear to awareness and let the love in us melt it away. Every time we can meet our fear with love — with forgiveness and loving kindness — we offer healing to all the world that still lives in fear.

Our practice of loving kindness is deepened immeasurably as we cultivate our capacity for self-acceptance. We'll explore this more deeply in the next chapter.

Loving Kindness Is a Fundamental Attitude

It is wiser to be kind than to be wise.

— NOAH benSHEA

The basis for loving kindness is a recognition, understanding, and appreciation of the shared and interdependent nature of our very being. Every living thing shares a longing to be happy and to be free from suffering. We all share the inherent worth of being part of creation. We all suffer the terrible pain of forgetfulness, the loss of the awareness of our perfection and wholeness, the fear and isolation that come with accepting the belief in separation and identifying with the ego.

Loving kindness is a fundamental attitude of mind, an openness of heart, that is expressed through us, through our thoughts, through our words, through our actions. It is not *what* we do, but *how* we do what we do. It is a sending of this message, spoken or not: "You are a holy and beloved child of God, completely deserving of love. You are my brother/sister, a part of myself. I wish for you only the happiness, peace, release from suffering, and remembrance of your true Self that I also wish for myself, and for all beings everywhere."

Loving kindness expresses the sincere and deep desire that we be healed back into the joy of our true nature. By offering loving kindness — by our willingness to meet and touch our own and others' suffering with mercy and love instead of fear and judgment — we begin to remember who we really are. As we offer healing, we are healed.

Shall we make a new rule of life from tonight:
Always to try to be a little kinder than is necessary?

— JAMES M. BARRIE

Chapter 3

Embracing Ourselves:
The Way of Self-Acceptance

In this, we discover a remarkable truth:
Much of spiritual life is self-acceptance,
if not all of it.

— Jack Kornfield, *A Path with Heart*

In the last chapter, we saw that the practice of loving kindness begins with ourselves. There is no more solid a foundation on which to build such love for ourselves — and for others as well — than the practice of *self-acceptance*. As we learn to open our hearts to ourselves, we discover a spaciousness within us that can hold everything — all that we are, all that life brings — in kindness, compassion, and love.

Accepting yourself is everything.
If you accept yourself,
you can accept the world.

— David Viscott

Self-acceptance is crucial to our healing. Our experience of separation cannot be undone if we are at war with ourselves. While we are judging, resisting, attacking, or fighting against anything within us, we cannot have a peaceful heart and mind. And this experience of inner conflict will inevitably be projected out into our relationships with others as well. What Jack Kornfield describes as "stopping the war within" is essential to experiencing harmony and peace in our outer lives as well.

The practice of self-acceptance has two aspects, or dimensions. The first of these is accepting that there is a deeper reality and potential to us that we can respect and aspire to realize. The second is accepting that we do not live from that deeper place in ourselves most of the time. Sogyal Rinpoche refers to this as beginning to respect ourselves as potential buddhas and at the same time recognizing our relative condition.

We can think of these two aspects as accepting our true potential (Self-acceptance) and accepting our ego (self-acceptance). Both are essential. In fact, it is the ground of Self-acceptance that makes real self-acceptance possible.

Self-Acceptance —
Accepting Our Potential

The goal of the spiritual journey is to reawaken to the truth of what we are, to let ourselves be restored to the awareness of our true identity as eternal spirit, as children of God, so that we may teach this identity by example and help others awaken as well. This awareness is already within us, and it dawns in our minds as we learn to see through and beyond all the illusory manifestations of separation that seem to deny it.

> *We are creation; we the Sons of God ... God's memory is in our holy minds, which know their oneness and their unity with their Creator. Let our function be only to let this memory return, only to let God's Will be done on earth, only to be restored to sanity, and to be but as God created us.*
>
> —W. p. 451; W-Pt.II.11.4:1, 5–6

To live as God created us, to dwell in and express the Self that is the deeper reality within us, is the source of our greatest possible joy and satisfaction in life. While in the deepest spiritual sense there is but one Self which is in us all, in this world we seem to be discrete and individual beings, and so this one Self will be manifest uniquely through each one of us. And within each of us, within every human being, this Self yearns for expression, calls to us for recognition, calls us to wake up and live.

The seed of God is in us. Given an intelligent and hard-working farmer, it will thrive and grow up to God, whose seed it is; and accordingly its fruits will be God-nature. Pear seeds grow into pear trees, nut seeds into nut trees, and God seed into God.

— MEISTER ECKHART

To say that the "seed of God" is within us should not be understood to mean that our divine nature is immature or undeveloped. God — our own Buddha nature or Christ nature — is already fully present and complete within us. What is undeveloped, what needs to be cultivated and matured, is our *awareness of,* and *identification with,* our God-nature.

As this awareness grows, as we grow and mature spiritually, we gradually let go of our ego identifications, of our sense of limitation and littleness in its many forms, and we live more and more from our true Self, our God-Self, from the abundance and fullness of our spiritual being.

*We are constantly invited
to be what we are.*

— HENRY DAVID THOREAU

If we are to grow the God-seed in us — to express and live from the best in ourselves — we need first to accept that this potential does, in fact, exist within us, and that it can be actualized. We must first accept that we *are* sons and daughters of God and that we can *live* as sons and daughters of God, here in this world.

To cultivate our awareness and experience of our inner divinity, to awaken to the God-seed of our own nature, we need to turn our attention away from the drama of the world and back into ourselves, into our hearts and minds. All mystical spiritual paths have taught that Heaven, or Enlightenment, or Truth, is to be found within. We need to turn within if we are to know ourselves and God.

The goal of awakening to, fulfilling, and living our God-nature may seem impossibly lofty. It may even seem pretentious or haughty to aspire to such a goal for ourselves. Poet e. e. cummings wrote, "It takes great courage to grow up and turn out to be who you really are," and in the ego-based world that certainly seems to be true. There is little support or agreement "out there" for aspiring to live our unique expression of greatness.

Yet if that greatness, that God-nature, is our true Self, can the purpose of our lives really be anything less than the realization and expression of that nature? And could we ever really be satisfied and content with anything less?

In a practical sense, what does it mean to accept this Self? *Self*-acceptance may begin simply by acknowledging that there are more of the qualities of God-nature within us than we normally express — more love, more compassion, more creativity, more forgiveness, more wisdom, more strength, more joy — and by accepting that we can develop and express these qualities more fully in our lives. To respond to the call of what we truly are is to be willing to commit ourselves to reaching for the highest and deepest potential within ourselves, for the fullest and richest potential of each moment of our lives.

To say yes to growing the God-seed within us means to be willing to look at and let go of the many ways we limit ourselves, choose pettiness, settle for being and expressing less than the son or daughter of God we really are. We look, not in order to judge or castigate ourselves, but so that we can recognize that we have the power to choose. Looking honestly at the choices we have made turns the present moment into a chance for us to choose again.

Accepting our true Self also means learning to appreciate and honor our own uniqueness. In this world, the Self can be expressed only through our individual selves. To accept and honor the Self means valuing and developing our talents and gifts as vehicles through which we can express love into the world. And it means being willing to contribute the best of who and what we are to life.

Accepting Our Own Talents and Gifts

The moment you accept yourself as you are, without any comparison, all inferiority, all superiority disappears. In that total acceptance of yourself you will be free from these complexes — inferiority, superiority. Otherwise you will suffer your whole life.... Just be yourself, and that's enough.

— OSHO, *Gold Nuggets*

In this world, we each have unique abilities, talents, and gifts. These are things that we are naturally drawn to do or express, things that feel like a part of us, activities with which we feel somehow at home. Although they may certainly involve effort and work, they are things that we enjoy, things that we love doing or expressing. These activities, these talents and gifts, are openings for God to be expressed through us into the world.

Someone once wrote that to enjoy life is to bring joy to life, to charge life with the energy and quality of joy. When we do things that we really enjoy doing, we become living instruments of joy. When we do things we truly love to do, we become channels for the flow of love. Expressing and utilizing our talents is a way in which we gift the world and the people around us.

The talents and gifts we have to bring to life are broad and varied. Some people have abilities and talents that are musical or artistic in nature. Some have a gift for expressing themselves in words. Some people are great cooks and love to entertain. Some

have a knack for gardening. Others have a talent for working with
their hands, for building or fixing things. Some people have a way
with children. Some are wonderful with animals.

Some people are "idea people," great at generating new ideas
and ways of doing things. Others are natural "doers," able to or-
ganize and follow through on projects and really get things done.
Some people are detail-oriented, good at intricate or precision
kinds of work. Some have a gift for seeing the "big picture," the
overview of a situation. Some people are natural leaders. Others
are great team players.

Some people are naturally funny and have a talent for making
others laugh. Some have a real gift for making other people feel
comfortable and good about themselves. Some are wonderful lis-
teners. Some people naturally inspire and empower others. Some
are unusually compassionate and kind.

The list could go on and on. Talents and gifts are abundant in
us. *Self*-acceptance includes acknowledging and respecting whatever your own talents are and recognizing that you can serve and
honor God by developing and expressing these gifts. We each have
a unique and essential place in the tapestry of creation, a place that
only we can fill. We fill that place by being fully who we are, by
letting love be expressed through our unique self.

We undermine this expression when we judge ourselves and
compare our own talents and abilities to those of others. Acceptance does not judge, nor does it compare. In order to develop
and cultivate our talents and gifts we must be willing not to judge
them. Rather we need to respect and honor them, appreciating
that they are part of our unique contribution to the whole of life
and creation.

*These roses under my window make no reference to former
roses or to better ones. They are what they are; they exist
with God today. There is no time to them. There is simply
the rose. It is perfect in every moment of its existence.*

— RALPH WALDO EMERSON

"Works in Progress" — Accepting Our Egos

*It is not the perfect but the imperfect
that is in need of our love.*

— Oscar Wilde

*Nothing is less important in life
than the score at halftime.*

— From a sign in a bar in Cairo, Ga.
(author unknown)

Acceptance of our deeper potential and the desire to manifest that potential is an expression of the quality of *aspiration*. Aspiration can be thought of as "spiritual stretching." It involves reaching beyond what we have already mastered, beyond the limitations with which we have identified, beyond what is already familiar and comfortable. Yet, as anyone who stretches as part of a physical exercise program understands, if stretching is to be integrated and assimilated it must not be harsh or forced. Rather it needs to be done gently and patiently, through a moment-to-moment practice of acceptance.

For a time I did a daily practice of hatha yoga. The *asanas,* or yoga postures, I worked with were designed to develop strength, flexibility, and balance. This practice was a wonderful classroom in which to work directly with the energies of both aspiration and acceptance. In each session I would have a clear image of what I aspired to — the full expression of each of the postures — and I would have my current level of accomplishment, which I needed to accept and work from. By accepting wherever I was in a given session as my starting point that day, continuing to aspire to mastery of the postures, treating myself with patience and gentleness, and practicing regularly, I made progress that was gradual but genuine. Even more important, I deepened my understanding and appreciation for the essential interplay of aspiration and acceptance in any arena of growth and developing mastery.

Few of us live consistently expressing the fullness of our true Self. Much of the time we give over to the limitations and little-ness of the ego, then add insult to injury by judging, criticizing, attacking, and rejecting ourselves for our human shortcomings, imperfections, and mistakes. We may tell ourselves we should be further along in our spiritual development than we are and feel disheartened about our path and practice. We may identify with our failures and feel unworthy or inadequate.

Each of these ways of treating or defining ourselves simply alienates us further from our real Self and deters us from cul-tivating and nurturing the God-seed within us. Just as we need to accept the divine potential that is in us, so we need to ac-cept where we are in the process of fulfilling and actualizing that potential. We must cultivate not only *Self*-acceptance but also *self*-acceptance. We need to accept ourselves as "works in progress," accept that we are in an ongoing process of growth and healing.

> *What I am to be, I am now becoming.*
> — BENJAMIN FRANKLIN

The ego often tries to convince us that we have to be perfect within this world, and then attacks us for falling short. But here in this world — within our humanity — we cannot be perfect. If that is what we insist upon for ourselves, we are bound to fail.

To develop the fullest potential and promise of our humanity, we need to give up our perfectionistic demands on ourselves. We need to be willing to accept, allow for, and even appreciate our imperfections and shortcomings.

Often it is through accepting our human weakness that our deeper strength, the strength of God within us, becomes revealed. Often it is through accepting our human shortcomings that we receive the experience of grace. We can appreciate our human imperfection as a window through which we might glimpse the workings of the indwelling God, of our deeper divine nature. We can ask for the sight that sees perfection beyond the imperfect appearance.

Native American cultures have a deep respect for the acceptance of our human imperfection. When weaving a rug, they will purposely include a flaw. This serves as a reminder that, while all that is humanly made is imperfect, it yet can reflect the beauty, reverence, care, and love of true creation.

Patience

Accepting ourselves as works in progress also means accepting the pace and tempo of our own growth and healing. It includes developing patience with ourselves and our process.

The foundation of patience, the Course teaches, is certainty of the outcome, certainty of eventual success. Real patience is not a state of passive waiting but of abiding in faith and in positive expectancy of the good that is certain to come in time.

> *Those who are certain of the outcome can afford to wait, and wait without anxiety. Patience is natural to the teacher of God. All he sees is certain outcome, at a time perhaps unknown to him as yet, but not in doubt.*
>
> —M. p. 13; M-4.VIII.1:1–3

There are times along the journey when reaching our destination seems way beyond reach. Like the hero Christian in John Bunyan's classic *Pilgrim's Progress,* we may feel ourselves slogging through, or sinking in, the "Slough of Despond" — the swamp of doubt and despair. We've all been in such places, and will most likely visit them again.

Yet fulfilling our spiritual destiny — *becoming* what we have been created to be — *cannot* be impossible. We are *destined* to become, to fully *be* in expression and experience, what we already are in the sight of God. We can delay, but that is all. Our Self is like a star, shining in the heavens of our own mind and heart, a star that will guide our journey home. We need only to set our sight on

it, commit ourselves to its course, and set out on our way — again
and again and again.

Wherever we are in our own process at this moment is fine, because it is a part of our learning and a step on our journey, and
will ultimately lead to the fulfillment of our potential and our purpose here. The Course teaches that there is a way of looking at
and understanding *everything* that happens in our experience here
that lets it be a step in our healing, a step toward God. This means
we cannot ever be in the wrong place. Wherever we are is a step
along the path toward our living in wholeness and joy, if we are
willing to view it and let it be used as such.

We progress along our path of growth and healing as we are
able, little by little, to let go of fear in its many forms and manifestations. The answer to fear is not more fear — judgment,
criticism, rejection, or threat. Fear is undone only by the gentle
touch of love.

Acceptance is the expression of unconditional love. It quietly
says, "You are worthy of love, just as you are, despite anything
you may think to the contrary, despite any judgments you may
have toward yourself." It affirms our true lovability, the love-
essence that we are, the seed of God that is within us. Acceptance
heals because it unites us with awareness of our Self, which is
wholly love.

Acceptance and Change

Acceptance is not a hopeless position;
it's the only position from which you can grow.

— David Viscott

Acceptance is less something we *do* than it is the natural outcome of what we *refrain from doing*. It is the state of being that
results from *not* judging, *not* comparing, *not* attacking, *not* saying, "This should be some other way." Acceptance is the natural

expression of love that simply lets things be as they are in this moment.

People sometimes fear that if they learn to accept themselves they will lose any motivation to grow or change. In fact, the opposite is true. Real change becomes possible only through self-acceptance.

Psychiatrist David Viscott describes clearly the effects of a lack of self-acceptance.

When you don't accept yourself, you become oversensitive to rejection.

When you don't accept yourself, you lose faith every time you trip over an old weakness.

When you don't accept yourself, you waste time looking for love to make you complete.

When you don't accept yourself, you try to beat others rather than seeking your best.

When you don't accept yourself, you overvalue material things.

When you don't accept yourself, you always feel lonely, and being with other people doesn't seem to help.

When you don't accept yourself, you live in the past....

When you don't accept yourself, you dread what each day may reveal about you.

When you don't accept yourself, the truth becomes your enemy.

When you don't accept yourself, you have no place to hide.

— DAVID VISCOTT, *Finding Your Strength in Difficult Times*

Acceptance is not the same as resignation. Resignation says that the way things are in this moment is the way they will be forever. True acceptance focuses only on the present moment and sets it free from the past. It sees the present as what is so *now* — as a starting point, fresh and vital and alive, a moment of possibility and choice. Thus it frees the future from the past, frees it to become an expression of something new, something that has not been manifest before.

Acceptance opens us to the possibility of transcendence or grace. When we stop denying, resisting, arguing or fighting with what is, we relax and open ourselves to a flow of creative energy through us that is otherwise blocked. We give up our attempts to control and manipulate and instead "let God be God" in us.

Accepting ourselves as "works in progress" simply means accepting that we still have egos. Ken Wapnick has often pointed out that "good" Course students are those who have come to terms with their own egos. This does not mean that we are to *identify* with the ego. It means we stop feeding it power and reality in our own minds by fighting it, resisting it, analyzing it, judging it, trying to overcome or get rid of it. We merely witness it with acceptance and love, and gently smile.

A wonderful teaching story is told about a dispute between the sun and the wind over who was more powerful. As they were arguing a man walked by wearing an overcoat. The wind and sun decided to hold a contest. Whoever could get the overcoat off the man first would be the more powerful of the two.

The wind began to bluster and blow. As the man felt the gusts, he gathered the front of his coat and pulled it tighter around him. The wind blew harder and the man drew his coat even tighter. The harder the wind blew, the more tenaciously the man held on and the more he resisted the blustery onslaught. Finally the wind exhausted himself and gave up in disgust.

The sun did nothing but shine. The day grew warmer, and the man as well. As the sun continued to shine its warmth and light, the man became so warm that he realized he did not need his overcoat. And so he simply took it off.

Most of what we dislike about ourselves, most of what we want to change in ourselves, is actually the ego defenses we've developed to try to handle our fears, insecurities, and negative feelings about ourselves. Often we go after our ego like the wind in this story. We bluster and blow at ourselves to change, to drop our defenses, to strip away and let go of our ego. But the more we try to *force* ourselves to give up our ego defenses and attachments, the tighter we seem to hold on to them.

Learning to accept ourselves is learning to be like the sun in the story. As we practice self-acceptance, as we learn to shine love on ourselves like the sun, we find that we begin to move naturally in the direction of ego relinquishment. In the light and warmth of patience and self-acceptance, our perceived need for our defenses begins to diminish. We become more willing and easily able to let them go. Change becomes natural, organic. Whatever energy and effort is required for change becomes an expression of caring for ourselves, instead of fighting against ourselves.

Fritz Perls, founder of Gestalt psychotherapy, called this the "paradoxical theory of change." Only when we accept ourselves fully, exactly as we are in this moment, is real change possible.

When we are able simply to accept that we have an ego, when we can step back and look at it without judgment, fear, or blame, something interesting happens. It begins to lose its hold on us. We discover that the ego is something that we *have* — a set of beliefs and defenses, a way of thinking and reacting — rather than being what we *are*. We become aware that there is also *something else* within us, a greater possibility and potential that we can choose to identify with and live from more and more.

Accepting the Shadow

The greatest challenge in the practice of self-acceptance lies in accepting what we consider to be most unacceptable in ourselves. Yet self-acceptance means accepting and including *all* of what we are and what we believe ourselves to be.

During my senior year in high school, I came upon what I decided in that moment would be my motto in life.

> Nihil humani mihi alienum est.
> *Nothing human is foreign to me.*
>   — TERENCE

At the time this was, for me, a deeply moving affirmation of the brotherhood and sisterhood of all humanity. Since then it has come to have an additional, perhaps more specific, meaning as well.

Each of us is an individualized expression of the whole of humanity, the whole of the human experience, at least in potential. This means that anything any human being can experience or do exists as a potential within me. If something exists *anywhere* within human nature, it exists within my own human nature as well.

Any act of inhumanity or cruelty, any atrocity committed or conceived by a human being exists as a potential within my own nature and being as well. There is no "them" who perpetrate the unspeakable. There is only us, only me. In the same way, there is no person or group of people whose triumphs of spirit, whose altruism, courage, greatness, and love, exist apart from and unreachable by the rest of us. If human beings do *anything,* then that thing is humanly possible — and therefore potential in me, in all of us.

In Eastern teachings there is a saying that everything that has a front has a back. In this world of separation, duality exists. Energy expresses itself in polarities, in opposites. Embracing ourselves as human beings means recognizing and accepting the polarities within our own consciousness. We contain both darkness and light, sorrow and joy, the capacity for selfishness as well as for generosity, for cruelty as well as compassion.

We often have a great fear of looking at the darkness within ourselves. Somehow we believe that if it is there, it must be who we *really* are, that our essential nature must be bad or evil. So we try to deny or hide from ourselves and the world any aspect of our "dark side." We judge and reject ourselves for feeling angry or afraid, weak or vulnerable, for thinking nasty or hateful or petty thoughts, for our passion and sexuality, for our emotional expressiveness, for being irrational, or lazy, or sloppy. This list goes on and on. The specifics may vary for each one of us, but we each have such a list.

We put on and present to the world what the Course calls the "face of innocence," or what Carl Jung called the *persona,* — a mask of what we consider "acceptable." We try to rid ourselves of what we consider the darkness in our minds, what Jung called the "shadow," — by denying and suppressing it, or by projecting what we reject in ourselves onto others. Yet the more we disown and defend against our shadow, the more fearful and convinced we become, on a deep level, that these shadow aspects must be the real truth of who we are.

The more we secretly believe the darkness to be the truth about ourselves, the harder we think we have to work to keep ourselves under control and the more afraid we become to be with ourselves and really look inside. We also avoid full and honest relationships with others, both to protect them against us and to protect ourselves against the darkness we suspect and fear may be at their core as well.

We may then "champion the light," not out of a free choice or deeper awareness of truth, but because we are so afraid of the dark. And we deny ourselves the opportunity to discover who we are at our essence, beyond all the polar manifestations of our egos, our personalities.

Jung has wisely written that we do not become enlightened by imagining figures of light, but by making the darkness conscious. Similarly, Stephen Levine has pointed out that we cannot attain Heaven by pushing away hell. The healing process is one of bringing the darkness in our minds to the gentle light of awareness. We need to reclaim our projections and look at all that we have feared to see within ourselves in the healing light of acceptance and love.

Each time we are willing to look at our shadow without judgment, with love, we open ourselves — and the whole of human consciousness — to healing. This inner work of healing is true service.

If you can imagine someone who is brave enough to withdraw all his projections, you get an individual who is aware of a considerable shadow. Such a man can no longer say

"they" do this or "they" must be fought against. Such a man
knows that whatever is wrong in the world is in himself and
if only he learns to deal with his own shadow, he is doing
something real for the world. He has succeeded in shoul-
dering at least an infinitesimal part of the gigantic unsolved
social problem of our day.

— CARL JUNG, *Man and His Symbols*

As we described in chapter 1, the Course refers to the process
of bringing our inner darkness to the light and looking at it clearly
without judgment or fear as "looking with the Holy Spirit." In
meditation practice it is called mindfulness. In transpersonal psychology, it is described as the process of developing the "inner
witness."

Developing the Inner Witness

We cultivate the state of consciousness described as the inner witness by learning to loosen our identification with the contents of
our consciousness, with any of the particular thoughts or feelings
or capacities within us. As we do we become aware of a perspective, or place in consciousness, from which we can recognize
and observe all the aspects and movements of our ego without
identifying ourselves as any one of them.

The quality of the inner witness can be illustrated through the
story of the six blind men and the elephant. Six blind men were
positioned along the length of an elephant and asked to describe
what an elephant is. The man at the tail said, "Ah, an elephant
is like a rope." The man at the hind leg said, "No, an elephant is
like a tree." The man at the side of the animal said, "An elephant
is like a great wall." The man at the front leg said, "An elephant
is like a pillar." The man at the trunk said, "An elephant is like a
hose." The man at the tusk said, "An elephant is like a sword."

None of these men was lying. Each was telling the truth of
his own experience. Yet none had the bigger picture, none had

the truth of what an elephant is. The witness perspective would be able to see the elephant, see the men, see how each man's description was "true" and "understandable" given his experience, and see that the reality or truth of elephant is none of these descriptions.

Developing the inner witness means being able to see how each aspect of our ego — including the most seemingly unacceptable ones — simply represents a limited, and thus distorted, perspective on reality. Each may even have a kind of subjective validity, but none has a clear picture of the truth. And none of these is who we really are.

The witness doesn't judge or analyze what it sees. It simply acknowledges all that is and holds it in compassionate awareness. The witness is the awakened awareness of the heart. It can experience any aspect or expression of our ego without identifying that as "self."

In and through cultivating the perspective of the witness, we can develop kindness and compassion for ourselves and move into unconditional love. Any thought, feeling, or experience can exist within us. As we loosen our identification with these contents of experience, we begin to sense our deeper being as awareness itself, as what Stephen Levine calls "the space in which these contents exist and float." We learn that we are not the ego, in any of its expressions or disguises.

A Daily Acceptance Practice

A few years ago, a close friend, teacher, and colleague of mine, Michael Melia, decided to take a stand in his life for complete self-acceptance. He developed and began working with a daily acceptance practice, which he found to be profoundly empowering and transformative. Here is a version of a daily acceptance practice that I adapted from his.

● ● ● ● ●

Begin by taking a few slow, deep breaths. With each breath, feel
the life force flowing through you, and let yourself relax gently
into the present moment. Say these words to yourself, silently or
aloud, and allow your heart to open to their full meaning:

I accept myself completely.
I accept my strengths and my weaknesses,
my gifts and my shortcomings,
my good points and my faults.
I accept myself completely as a human being.

I accept that I am here to learn and grow,
and I accept that I am learning and growing.
I accept the personality I've developed,
and I accept my power to heal and change.
I accept myself without condition or reservation.
I accept that the core of my being is goodness
and that my essence is love,
and I accept that I sometimes forget that.
I accept myself completely, and in this acceptance
I find an ever-deepening inner strength.
From this place of strength, I accept my life fully
and I open to the lessons it offers me today.

I accept that within my mind are both fear and love,
and I accept my power to choose which
I will experience as real.
I recognize that I experience only the results
of my own choices.
I accept the times that I choose fear
as part of my learning and healing process,
and I accept that I have the potential and power
in any moment to choose love instead.
I accept mistakes as a part of growth,
so I am always willing to forgive myself
and give myself another chance.

I accept that my life is the expression of my thought,
and I commit myself to aligning my thoughts
more and more each day with the Thought of Love.
I accept that I am an expression of this Love,
Love's hands and voice and heart on earth.
I accept my own life as a blessing and a gift.
My heart is open to receive, and I am deeply grateful.
May I always share the gifts that I receive
fully, freely, and with joy.
Amen.

I invite you to work with this practice for a time — perhaps six months — or to write and work with one of your own. If you will allow this message of self-acceptance and forgiveness to begin to permeate your relationship with yourself, the changes in how your life feels to you will be dramatic and far-reaching.

As you work with this practice, or one like it, there may well be times when ego resistance is strong. The ego itself is a thought of judgment and nonacceptance. Acceptance is therefore perceived by the ego as a threat. Resistance to the practice may express itself as disbelief about what you are saying, cynical rebuttals, feelings of anxiety, discomfort, and unworthiness, a harsh litany of self-accusation and attack, boredom, or in a variety of other ways. As best you can, simply witness these resistances as they arise, breathe, and let your heart be open and tender toward your fear. Then gently continue with the practice.

There is a place in you where the words of this practice are already true. There is a place in you where you already hold yourself in total acceptance and love. Saying these words with sincere intention helps you naturally move toward that place in yourself. Doing this type of practice expresses your willingness and commitment to join with and live from that kindness and love.

As we practice and deepen self-acceptance, we begin to develop both compassion and respect for ourselves as human beings. We develop compassion for our own suffering, for our human limitations and shortcomings. And we develop respect for our deeper possibilities, for our capacity to reach beyond ourselves, and for our courage to love and grow and meet our lives with openness and truth.

Opening to Others

The love of our neighbor in all its fullness
simply means being able to say to him,
"What are you going through?"

— SIMONE WEIL

The way we treat ourselves inevitably spills over into how we treat others. As we open more and more to accepting and embracing the whole of what we are, we can also open to deeper, more authentic contact and relationship with others. As we open the space in ourselves where we can hold in love and compassion the full range of our own human experience, we can also make room for another's experience — for, whatever it is, it will not threaten us. We can let others be, and we can be with them.

In my counseling work, I have found that often the deepest longing people have — and the most profound healing they experience — is simply to have the space to be human, with another human being and with themselves. Quietly and simply, this is the experience of love. And love is what heals our painful sense of separation, of being alone. Love holds us gently in the arms of acceptance, wholeness, and peace.

Years ago, when I first began practicing counseling, I came across a passage in a novel called *The Women's Room* that transformed my understanding of therapy and healing. The main character in the book was a middle-aged woman whose tidy suburban life fell apart when her husband left her for a younger woman. She set out to rebuild her life by going back to college.

She found that many of her new young friends were coming to her with their problems, and she felt very puzzled by that. How could she possibly be of help to anyone, she wondered, when she had made such a mess of her own life? Yet, in reflecting on her interactions with these friends, she realized that she had, in fact, helped.

> *She had helped, listening. She had not denied their truths. She had not asked, by flicker or gesture, that they censor themselves. She had not insisted that they be happy people with happy problems.... All she had done was, unblinking and uninterrupting, let them be whatever horrid creature they thought they were....*
>
> *The idea seemed a great truth when it descended upon her around four in the morning: a space to be and a witness.... It was enough, or if not enough, it was all, all that we could do, in the end, for each other.*
>
> — MARILYN FRENCH, *The Women's Room*

In research on the near-death experience, a common element discovered in the experience is what is sometimes called the "life review." In the presence of a Being of pure love, the person witnesses every moment and event of his or her life. There is not judgment but only understanding and acceptance of the lessons offered by those events. There is also an experience of empathy and compassion for everyone who played a part in the person's life — an ability to see things from their perspective. The life review is universally described as profoundly comforting and healing by those who have experienced it.

The elements of the life review offer a beautiful summary of the healing process we can offer to each other. To bear compassionate witness — in a heart-space of nonjudgment, acceptance, and love — to another's human experience, to recognize that we walk beside others on this journey of human life, to hold a safe space in which they can be open to the lessons being offered them and forgive themselves and others is perhaps, after all, the most we can do for one another.

It is not up to you to change your brother,
but merely to accept him as he is.

—T. p. 156; T-9.III.6:4

Our human relationships are the setting in which we can learn to offer and share this healing. We grow through our willingness to learn how to forgive ourselves and each other our human imperfections.

Acceptance does not mean we have to tolerate behavior from others that may be humanly hurtful to us or to themselves. It does mean that we learn to set whatever limits are needed with love and compassion instead of hatred and fear. And we learn to see past all the manifestations of our egos, all the apparent outer differences that seem to separate us, to the love that still lives deep in our hearts. Sharing this love with each other and the world is truly our greatest joy and deepest fulfillment in life.

Beyond all of our seeming differences, we are, at our core, the same. Acknowledging what we share, we come to remember we are not alone. In this lies the greater healing, the greater release from suffering. And in this recognition of our sameness, compassion is born in our hearts.

Chapter 4

Compassion

I promise to relieve the suffering of others.

You can hold yourself back from the suffering of the world: this is something you are free to do ... but perhaps precisely this holding back is the only suffering you might be able to avoid.

— FRANZ KAFKA

What do we live for if it is not
to make life less difficult for each other?

— GEORGE ELIOT

Compassion is the fundamental stance described in the promise to "relieve the suffering of others." Compassion is the natural outpouring of the heart that wants to heal, to relieve suffering and replace it with comfort and peace. It is our natural response to suffering and pain.

The love in our hearts hears in all suffering a cry for love, a cry for help, and reaches out to answer that cry. There is a deep wisdom to love that we can trust and count on. When we are centered in and responding from that wisdom, we will automatically answer the cries for love we hear in a way that is appropriate and genuinely helpful.

Shared Suffering, Shared Healing

Do you not think the world needs peace as much as you do?
Do you not want to give it to the world as much as you want
to receive it? For unless you do, you will not receive it.

—T. p. 134; T-8.IV.4:1–3

The first Noble Truth of the Buddha is that life in this world is suffering. Suffering is born of and tends to reinforce our experience of separation. Our pain seems very much our own and seems to isolate us and make us different from those around us who do not seem to be hurting. Yet whatever any one of us suffers is, in fact, part of the greater suffering shared by the whole family of creation.

Whatever our pain — whether it is physical, emotional, mental, or spiritual — somewhere in this world other living beings are, at this very moment, suffering the same kind of pain. Someone else is feeling the same pain of a toothache, or back spasm, or cancer. Someone else is suffering the same pain of loneliness, loss, a betrayed or broken heart. Someone else is suffering the same mental torment of regret, worry, indecision, or fear. Someone else is suffering the same gnawing sense of unworthiness, doubt, or spiritual darkness.

Beyond *our* pain and suffering is *the* pain and suffering experienced by all living, feeling beings. As we begin to recognize this level of shared suffering, genuine compassion is born in us.

At the deepest level, all of the specific forms of pain we experience in this life reflect the profound suffering generated by our belief that we are separate from God and from each other. The belief in separation gives rise to the terrible pain of feeling alone, unloved, judged, abandoned, bereft, or afraid that everyone has experienced in some form as part of our human, separated condition.

Compassion always speaks in some way to this deepest level of suffering. It always carries the healing message, "You are not alone. You are worthy of love, and you are loved." However this is communicated — through words or touch, through practical kinds of help, through encouragement and support, through prayers for healing — what really heals, what truly relieves the suffering, is the love we offer and share.

> *And remember, we all stumble, every one of us.*
> *That's why it's a comfort to go hand in hand.*
>
> — E. K. BROUGH

Compassion rests on the recognition that just as we all share the same source of suffering, we all share the same need for healing. We all need to awaken from the nightmare of separation and fear. We all share the need and longing for release from pain. Literally, when I look upon another's suffering, no matter the form, I am looking at my own call for help and healing. My response to my brother or sister is my answer to myself.

When I help another, when I teach another that he or she is not alone and friendless in this world, I offer myself the same happy, healing lesson. As the Course teaches over and over again, what I give to my brother or sister is my gift to myself. As I give of the love in my heart, I open to experience more fully the comforting presence and reality of that love.

Judgment — the Block to Compassion

If compassion is our natural response to suffering, why is it that we do not respond more often to the suffering we see all around us with an unreserved, unhesitating extension of love? Why so often do we turn away rather than reach out to relieve the suffering of others? What blocks our experience and expression of compassion?

The major block to compassion is the judgment in our minds. Judgment is the mind's primary tool of separation. Stephen Levine describes judgment as "the cold wind in the abyss between the heart and the mind." The Course states that "the choice to judge ... is the cause of the loss of peace" (T. p. 45; T-3.VI.2:1).

Levine contrasts compassion, or mercy, with judgment.

Mercy is the opposite of judgement. It is a heartfelt opening rather than a mindless closing.... Mercy unites; judgement separates. Mercy is the voice of the unitive, of our "natural goodness."... Mercy does not judge its own absence. It is open even to our closedness. Judgement regards everything with an equal mercilessness. Judgement wounds; mercy heals.

— STEPHEN LEVINE, *Guided Meditations,*
Explorations, and Healings

Judgment declares something or someone to be undeserving of love and is thus a barrier to the experience and expression of love. Love does not judge, for it sets up no barriers to its own extension. We cannot judge and be centered in love. We cannot judge others' suffering and be compassionate toward them. If on any level we view their suffering as deserved or justified, we cannot offer them true healing. We cannot help to relieve their suffering by adding to their belief in it.

Judgment can be subtle in its operation. It may not always take the form of overt condemnation or blame. It may take the form of making outer differences real and using them to reinforce the belief in and experience of separateness and isolation. Judgment sees the one who suffers as different from and somehow less than the one who does not.

Such a stance is born, not out of love, but out of our fear of confronting our own suffering. Because we are afraid of it, we want to see it as separate and apart from us. When we deny our own suffering, we also deny our need for healing. This gives rise to the emotion of *pity*, or feeling sorry for someone, which is sometimes confused with true compassion and mercy.

> *Mercy is defined by some as pity, but pity is born of fear — it wishes not to experience the pain of another or of oneself. When we touch pain with fear, that is pity. When we fear our own pain, that is self-pity. But when we touch pain with love — that is mercy. Mercy is a blessing. Pity is a hindrance.*
>
> — STEPHEN LEVINE, *Guided Meditations,*
> *Explorations, and Healings*

Pity is a hindrance to healing because fear is a denial of love. Pity denies the power of love to relieve all suffering by seeing suffering as something other than our shared call for love. By not recognizing the suffering of others as a call for love and responding to them with love, we miss hearing and responding to our own call as well. We delay our own healing each time we judge, each time we withhold our love.

Compassion, Charity, and Remembrance of God

Compassion, on the other hand, is an expression of a *charitable* attitude toward others and ourselves. We open our hearts, we see with a deeper vision, through eyes of love. Love's vision sees past all the appearances that reflect our lostness and confusion and forgetfulness to the place within us that still remembers what we really are. Charity recognizes in the present that one day we will be restored to full awareness of the truth in us. Compassion seeks only to help that process of remembering.

> *Charity is a way of looking at another as if he had already gone far beyond his accomplishments in time.... The char-*

*ity that is accorded him is both an acknowledgment that he
needs help, and a recognition that he will accept it.*

—T. p. 23; T-2.V.10:1, 3

Jesus in the Course and the *boddhisattvas* in the Buddhist tradition are models of charity and compassion. Having themselves
seen through the veil of illusion, they reach out to help us on our
journey toward awakening. Not giving the power of credence to
the fearful illusions we still believe, they offer us the strength of
their certainty that we will join them in laying illusions aside and
waking to joy. They remember who we are, though we still forget.
In their remembering, ours is fully accomplished and awaits only
our acceptance of it in time.

We can follow the example of these great teachers and guides.
We can learn to see and honor the divine potential within everyone — what in Buddhist tradition is called our Buddha nature —
and we can reflect this reality to one another through the mirror of
our loving hearts. In this lies our own remembrance and healing.

*You forsake yourself and God if you forsake any of your
brothers. You must learn to see them as they are, and understand they belong to God as you do.*

—T. p. 76; T-5.IV.6:6–7

As we are willing to practice compassion — as we are willing
to see another's suffering and need for healing as our own and to
offer another the healing love we would ourselves receive — we
remember that we are children of God, beloved by our Creator.
As we teach our brothers and sisters that they are not alone, we
remember that we are not alone. We remember God's love for us
as we let that love reach through us to bless one whom we had
seen as separate and apart. We join with others in our mind and
heart, seeing them as a part of ourselves, welcoming them home
to love. And so we are released with them from the suffering that
separation brings.

Compassion Is Love among Equals

Compassion is the spontaneous and natural response to suffering offered by a loving heart and a mind unclouded by judgment and fear. It grows out of a deep recognition of our basic sameness and *equality*. It is the willingness to see beyond the outer appearance of differences — to perceive "the universal mark of God" (T. p. 3; T-1.I.40:2) that unites us in love — that allows us to reach out to others in ways that truly alleviate suffering. This is what the Course refers to as working miracles, or offering true healing. Miracles release us from suffering by undoing its real cause: the belief in separation, inequality, and difference.

> *The miracle is a sign of love among equals.*
> — T. p. 5; T-1.II.3:4

We have already drawn a distinction between pity and compassion. Pity holds another's suffering at a distance, sees it as separate and apart from us. It is born out of our fear of confronting our own deep suffering and need for healing. Pity is the ego's parody of compassion and emphasizes the difference between the one who seems to suffer and the one who does not. It reinforces a belief in inequality. It makes a proclamation, whether covert or blatant, of superiority and inferiority.

> *Most of what passes muster as pity*
> *is actually disguised gloating.*
> — Fritz Perls

Action taken out of pity, out of feeling sorry for someone, can never truly heal nor genuinely alleviate suffering. While it may temporarily help relieve the outer expression of a problem, it fundamentally serves to strengthen and reinforce the underlying cause. It mires us, together, deeper into the suffering we all share.

What truly heals the suffering of our separated existence is not the actions we take, in and of themselves, but rather what we *ex-*

press through these actions. If they are truly compassionate — that
is, if they are genuine expressions of love and of the recognition
of our essential unity — they will relieve suffering by healing its
cause. Yet the very same actions, done without love, may treat the
symptom while actually deepening the root of the pain.

Compassion and Action:
"First Remove the Log from Your Own Eye"

In *Seeking the Heart of Wisdom,* Jack Kornfield raises a question
that must at one time or another be faced by all those who follow a spiritual path that teaches that this world is illusory, empty,
unreal. He writes,

> *One of the most important questions we come to in spiritual
> practice is how to reconcile service and responsible action in
> the world with a meditative life based on nonattachment, let-
> ting go, and coming to understand the empty nature of all
> conditioned things. Are the values we hold that lead us to
> giving and serving and caring for one another different from
> the values that lead us deep within ourselves on the journey
> of liberation and awakening?*
>
> — JACK KORNFIELD, "THE PATH OF SERVICE,"
> IN JOSEPH GOLDSTEIN AND JACK KORNFIELD,
> *Seeking the Heart of Wisdom*

One of the criticisms sometimes leveled against the Course is
the mistaken assertion that it encourages apathy and discourages
participation in the world because it teaches that all healing is
accomplished through the changing of our own minds and perceptions. The Course does, in fact, ask that we "seek not to change
the world but choose to change [our] mind[s] about the world"
(T. p. 415; T-21.Intro.1:7). But it is helpful to look at this teaching
more closely.

The change of mind that the Course is asking us to choose is a
healing of our minds, a release from judgment and fear. We are

asked to take responsibility for what we have individually and collectively projected onto the world, for all the fearful images of guilt, attack, devastation, and horror that exist in our own minds. We are asked to bring our judgment and fear to the light of aware-ness, the presence of love within us, where such thoughts can be gently corrected, dispelled. As fear and judgment dissolve, we are able to look upon the world with the clear-sighted vision of love.

This change of mind and perception is what the Course defines as a miracle, or a shift into right-mindedness. The Course also states that "miracles...induce action" (T. p. 5; T-1.II.2:4). Love seeks expression. In this world, the voice for love in our hearts may direct us toward compassionate participation and action.

The Course is certainly not against such action. But it is quite clear that wrong-minded, or ego-based, action is inherently and inevitably misguided and therefore cannot be truly helpful.

This teaching is also expressed in the Gospel of Matthew (7:3–5). In this passage, Jesus asks why we are so concerned with removing a speck from our brother's eye when there is a log in our own. How can we possibly know how to effectively help our brother while our own perception is distorted and obscured? First, Jesus tells us, we need to remove the log from our own eye. Then we will see clearly how to remove the speck from our brother's eye. It is not that we are not to reach out to one another, to help each other. But we cannot see how best to help until we remove whatever is distorting and blocking our own clarity of vision.

The log in our own eye is all the judgments, fears, ego invest-ments, and grievances we are holding on to. The ego loves to tell us what someone else's problem is and what should be done to correct it. But it will always be wrong, because it is looking only from its own separate, limited, partial — and therefore dis-torted — point of view. The ego never sees the whole picture and therefore never sees accurately and clearly. Only as we are willing to remove the log — to relinquish our egocentric ideas of what is wrong and how to help and to open instead to love's direc-tion, to the perception and guidance of the deeper wisdom of our hearts — can we take action that is truly compassionate, action that will bring healing and release from separation and suffering to everyone concerned.

> *What would You have me do?*
> *Where would You have me go?*
> *What would You have me say, and to whom?*
>   —W. p. 121; W-Pt.I.71.9:3–5

The action we are guided to take once we have removed the log may be a physical or tangible reaching out, it may be a reaching out at the level of mind such as through prayer, or it may even appear to be no action. The essential thing is that it is not we ourselves who make that decision, but rather the love in our hearts and minds that directs us. If we are listening to love, we will take action that is genuinely helpful and appropriate. Love's healing touch will naturally express itself in the form in which it can best be received and accepted (T. p. 20; T-2.IV.5).

Does this mean that we have to stop each time we feel inclined to reach out to someone, to offer help in any way, and check our motivations through meditation or prayer? Both Buddhism and the Course are paths that emphasize practical wisdom in our lives and our journey of spiritual growth. We need not become obsessed with whether our motivation is entirely ego-free in every single thing we decide or do. We simply need to be willing to use the times that our egos are *obviously* involved, the times that we are not at peace, to practice changing our minds, asking for a miracle, removing the log from our own eye first.

When we are confused about whether or how to help, when we feel any conflict about giving, when we feel uneasy or fearful about someone's situation, when we feel pity or contempt for another, when we feel guilty over another's difficulty or pain, when we become judgmental of ourselves or others, or self-righteous about our own position — these are the times we need to stop, turn within, ask for help. At such times, we need to receive healing, to recenter in love, before we can offer healing to another. It is this recognition that restores us to an awareness of our equality with each other, of our shared need for healing, and ultimately of our shared reality as love.

The Way of Service

One of the most beautiful expressions of compassion I know is the Prayer of St. Francis:

> *Lord, make me an instrument of your peace;*
> *where there is hatred, let me sow love.*
> *where there is injury, pardon;*
> *where there is doubt, faith;*
> *where there is despair, hope;*
> *where there is darkness, light;*
> *and where there is sadness, joy.*
>
> *O Divine Master,*
> *grant that I may not so much seek*
> *to be consoled as to console;*
> *to be understood as to understand;*
> *to be loved as to love;*
> *for it is in giving that we receive,*
> *and it is in pardoning that we are pardoned,*
> *and it is in dying [to self] that we are born*
> *into eternal life.*

This prayer expresses, not only a profound dedication and devotion to love, but also a deep understanding of the relationship between our own spiritual awakening and reaching out in healing service to others.

Through the path of conscious service compassion can be cultivated, expressed, and deepened. Thus service offers us a tangible way to practice and learn oneness in our daily lives.

Chapter 5

Love, and Do What You Will: The Way of Service

Right where we are, in whatever we're already doing, the op-portunity to be of service is almost always present.... All we have to do is ask, "How can I help?" with an open heart, and then really listen.

— RAM DASS AND PAUL GORMAN, *How Can I Help?*

One of the ways we can deepen the practice of compassion in our lives is through consciously walking the path of service. The choice to be of service naturally grows out of our sense of com-passion — the desire to help alleviate the suffering of others — and out of the understanding that our own healing, happiness, and well-being are inextricably bound together with that of others. Service is an arena of experience in which we can develop, prac-tice, and deepen our awareness that we are not separate from each other but are joined deeply in our common humanity and our shared divinity.

No matter what our personal path to God, service is always a necessary step on the path. The meditator must rise from his pillow to share what he has seen within himself. The stu-

dent of Truth must teach what he has learned, by living it.
The lover of God must love the God within his brothers
and sisters. Awakening is useless unless it awakens the world;
wisdom is useless unless it is lived; and love is fruitless unless
it is given.

— ALAN COHEN, *The Dragon Doesn't Live Here Anymore*

Service is a necessary step on the path because it is, in a very
real way, inseparable from where and how we live our daily lives.
We live in this world with other people, and the "dailyness" of our
lives is very much made up of *encounter* and *relationship* — from
the casual, passing, seemingly chance encounters with strangers on
the subway, in the check-out line at the grocery store, or riding in
the elevator, to the interactions of our work and social relationships, friendships, love and family relationships. Service cannot be
separated from relationship and, in a very real sense, relationship
cannot be separated from service.

Susan Trout, cofounder and director of the Institute for Attitudinal Studies in Washington, D.C., points out that there are two
levels on which we serve others.

First, we are all unconsciously and unintentionally in a con-
stant state of service through the example of our lives. As we
become more conscious of this level of service, and as we de-
velop our own inner peace, we move into the second level of
service in which service becomes an act of intention from the
heart. At this level, service manifests as love in action.

— SUSAN TROUT, *To See Differently*

Service can thus be understood both as a *state of being* and as
love in action. Intentional, or purposeful, service includes being
committed to developing our inner peace, our ability to live centered in love, and then letting that peace and love be expressed and
be shared with others through action and interaction.

Service as a State of Being

We live not only for ourselves. A thousand fibers connect us with our fellow-men; and along those fibers, as sympathetic threads, our actions run as causes, and they come back to us as effects.

— HERMAN MELVILLE

Service begins, in a sense, with the basic awareness that our lives and well-being are genuinely and inextricably connected to the lives and well-being of others. The Course describes a teacher of God as anyone who has in some way recognized that his or her own interests are not separate from those of someone else.

Out of the awareness of our fundamental interconnectedness comes a recognition that we are in a state of constant service to each other. We cannot help but affect one another by our thoughts, attitudes, moods, words, and actions.

I am alone in nothing. Everything I think or say or do teaches all the universe. A Son of God cannot think or speak or act in vain. He cannot be alone in anything.

—W. pp. 87–88; W-Pt.I.r.I.54.4:2–5

The Course teaches that there are *no chance meetings* in our lives. Everyone we meet, every encounter, no matter how seemingly casual or passing, is part of the Holy Spirit's plan for our healing, part of what the Course calls our special function. And, in some way, whether obvious or subtle, we will touch and be touched in every encounter we have with anyone.

One of the loveliest descriptions of the awareness of this interconnectedness that I've come across was shared by Peggy Millin in *Mary's Way*, an account of her pilgrimage to Medjugorje.

I was on a train on a rainy day. The train was slowing down to pull into a station. For some reason I became intent on watching the raindrops on the window. Two separate drops, pushed by the wind, merged into one for a moment and then divided again — each carrying with it a part of the other. Simply by that momentary touching, neither was what it had been before. And as each one went on to touch other raindrops, it shared not only itself, but what it had gleaned from the other. I saw this metaphor many years ago and it is one of my most vivid memories. I realized then that we never touch people so lightly that we do not leave a trace. Our state of being matters to those around us, so we need to become conscious of what we unintentionally share so we can learn to share with intention.

— PEGGY TABOR MILLIN, *Mary's Way*

Every relationship we have, every interaction with anyone, is a *teaching-learning situation.* We both teach and learn who we are, and what life and the world are like, through our interactions and relationships with others.

The Course makes clear that we are all teaching all the time, and that we teach primarily by *example,* by what we ourselves embody. We do not have a choice about whether or not we teach. We have a choice only about *what* we teach. In this there are two, and only two, possibilities. We will teach either fear or love, separation or unity, in every relationship, every interaction, every encounter we have. And, the Course points out, we will *learn* exactly what we teach.

Service, at its deepest core, is an *intention* we bring to a relationship. It is an inner choice we make to have the relationship serve a helpful and healing purpose. While in outer form it may sometimes appear that one person is the helper and the other is the one being helped, deeper insight and understanding reveal that in any relationship of true service help is always mutual, healing always shared. For healing by its very nature involves the dissolution of our sense of separateness and isolation, our feelings of being different and alone. We discover in their place our common humanity, this journey we share, the love and unity that we somehow know to be our true essence and home.

Thus service can be thought of, not as limited to certain specialized kinds of activities, settings, or kinds of relationships, but rather as a *continual focus* to our living. It is an ongoing path and practice of choosing a state of mind and being that expresses love rather than distrust and fear, that recognizes what we share as human beings and as sons and daughters of God rather than focusing on what separates us and would make us strangers to one another. Service is the choice to reach beyond the comfort zones, defenses, and confines of our egos to meet as equals in the deeper space of the heart. We remind one another of the spiritual identity we share, and in this reminding we are healed together.

This state of mind and being needs to be practiced and cultivated if it is to be lived. In this world we spend most of our time and energy defending and preserving our ego identities, our seemingly separate interests and concerns. The internal shift, the change of mind, from an ego-centered, fear-based perspective to a spiritual, love-based perception and awareness is, again, what the Course means by a miracle. And, the Course points out:

> *A miracle is a service. It is the maximal service you can render to another. It is a way of loving your neighbor as yourself. You recognize your own and your neighbor's worth simultaneously.*
>
> —T. p. 2; T-1. I.18

The real focus of service, then, is on what we choose to offer others through our minds and hearts, through our consciousness and being. The Course teaches that minds naturally communicate. Actions and behaviors are a *means* for communication, not ends in and of themselves. The same action can communicate either judgment and fear or joining and love, depending on the thought and motivation from which it derives.

True service is found in the choice to communicate love, to be an expression of and transparency for love. In that choice we become, like St. Francis, instruments of peace, instruments of help and healing.

Service as Love in Action

The nature of love is to extend, and we said earlier that a second meaning of service is *love in action*. What we always need to remember with respect to helping and service is that for any action to be truly helpful, we first need to be centered in love. The miracle — the inner shift by which we join with the love in our minds and hearts rather than with our ego — must come first. Otherwise any action we take will inevitably be misguided.

Our deeper vision, our intuitive knowing of how to be truly helpful, is blocked and distorted by our prejudices and judgments, our overt and hidden guilt and fears, our need for specialness, our arrogance in believing we know what is needed or what is best in a given situation. When we are caught up in any of these forms of wrong-minded thought, we are disconnected from the love and natural wisdom in our hearts and minds. We cannot be of real help and service from such a place in our consciousness.

When we jump into trying to help or serve from a wrong-minded perspective, we become like Martha in the Gospel of Luke.

> *In the course of their journey he came to a village, and a woman named Martha welcomed him into her house. She had a sister called Mary, who sat down at the Lord's feet and listened to him speaking. Now Martha who was distracted with all the serving said, "Lord, do you not care that my sister is leaving me to do all the serving by myself? Please tell her to help me." But the Lord answered: "Martha, Martha," he said, "you worry and fret about so many things, and yet few are needed, indeed only one. It is Mary who has chosen the better part; it is not to be taken from her."*
>
> — LUKE 10:38–42

When we "serve" for the wrong reasons, when our action comes out of worry, obligation, seeking approval, or any other ego-based motives, we will inevitably find ourselves sooner or later feeling separate, resentful, unappreciated, taken advantage of, even burnt out. Jesus tells us that the "better part" — that is, what must take priority for us, the one thing that we really need to do — is to listen to and be guided by the Voice for love within us.

What is asked of us is a willingness on our part to look at and release the blocks and interferences to love within ourselves. As we do, we reconnect with inner guidance that knows how love can be best expressed at any given moment, in any given situation. We can trust that whatever we do when we are inwardly joined with love will offer healing. That is why St. Augustine taught, "Love, and do what you will."

Service as a Spiritual Curriculum

While service is not limited to formally defined helping situations or relationships, intentionally chosen service can be a particularly accelerated healing curriculum. The path of service provides fertile soil for our personal growth, and our personal growth increases our capacity to be of real service. Each time we allow ourselves to move beyond illusions of separation in our own minds, experience, and relationships, we advance the healing of the Sonship as a whole — in ways, the Course tells us, we can neither imagine nor comprehend.

We have already said that true service calls us to reach beyond our limited sense of self, beyond the comfort zones of our ego. In the process it brings us face to face with the outer edges of those comfort zones, with our resistances and fears, our defenses and feelings of vulnerability, with the places we shut down and close our hearts. It shows us where we are in need of healing, where we need to grow and expand our sense of who and what we are.

It also offers us a clear and wonderful opportunity to move beyond those limitations and ego-based comfort zones to discover deeper resources of compassion, caring, understanding, and wisdom that are within us. We learn that we are more than we thought we were, and we discover that in love, generosity, and giving we feel most truly ourselves.

And when we meet heart-to-heart at a place beyond the surface appearances that make one of us the helper and the other the one being helped, we discover a fulfillment, recognition, and joy in that joining that teaches us unity is our real home.

Making a Difference

In the Middle East there is a legend of a little sparrow lying on its back in the middle of the road. A horseman comes by, dismounts and asks the sparrow why it is lying upside down like that.

"I hear the heavens are about to fall today," says the sparrow.

"Oh," says the horseman, "and I suppose your puny legs can hold up the heavens?"

"One does what one can," replies the sparrow. "One does what one can."

— Quoted by Ruth Fishel
in *5 Minutes for World Peace...Forever*

A guru once said that it is easy to be spiritual meditating in a cave or on a mountain, surrounded by the beauty and peacefulness of nature. But to be able to be centered, awake, and peaceful in the middle of New York City — *that,* he said, is spiritual *graduate school.*

One of the most difficult things about living in a large city — or in watching the evening news or reading the newspaper — is being confronted with the enormity of human suffering that exists all around us: poverty, homelessness, drugs, bigotry, violence, illness, the isolation of the elderly, the terrible loneliness that permeates the lives of so many people.

It is very clear that much more is needed in our world than any one of us can possibly do or give. And in the face of that reality there is also a tendency to pull back, to protect ourselves, to preserve our boundaries and avoid being overwhelmed by the suffering or by our own sense of despair and futility. Nearly everyone, and especially those on a conscious path of compassion and service, must at one time or another struggle with this dilemma — wanting deeply to help, but wondering if our efforts really make a difference anyway.

I once heard Gerald Jampolsky tell the following story: A man was walking along a beach in Hawaii after a storm. Hundreds and hundreds of starfish had been washed ashore during the storm and stranded on the sand. They were certain to die before the next high tide could carry them back out to sea. The man thought to himself how tragic this situation was, that all these starfish were going to die, and kept on walking. As he rounded a bend, he saw another man on the beach, picking up starfish and throwing them back into the water.

The first man approached the second and said to him, "There are hundreds, thousands of starfish here. You can't possibly save them all. Don't you realize that what you're doing doesn't make any difference?"

The second man didn't reply. He simply reached down, picked up a starfish, and threw it back into the sea. "Made a difference to that one," he said.

> *Nobody could make a greater mistake*
> *than he who did nothing*
> *because he could only do a little.*
>
> — EDMUND BURKE

Dr. Jampolsky shares that he once asked Mother Teresa how she was able to deal with opening her door morning after morning and being confronted with a vast ocean of human need and misery. Mother Teresa responded that she simply takes one person at a time, does whatever she can to help the one she is with, and trusts that in her efforts to serve God's children she is not alone.

Some years ago a man in one of my study groups, a New York City police detective, described how he'd come to terms with the question of making a difference in his work. He too was faced with an enormity of suffering and horror each day. He had gone back to the example of Jesus in the Gospels for guidance. He noticed that Jesus always did what he could for those who asked for his help. He did *not* say to his disciples, "Go out and round up all the lepers you can find and bring them here to me so I can heal them all." Like Mother Teresa, Jesus had simply helped the one who was right in front of him and knew without a doubt that he was not alone.

Each of us living in this world must come to terms with if, how, and how much we want to, and can, help. Around Thanksgiving in 1988, I attended a concert at the Cathedral of St. John the Divine to raise money and awareness regarding homelessness in New York City. Ram Dass, one of the organizers of the event, told this story: A pig and a chicken were out walking together one morning and wanted to have some breakfast. They passed a little roadside diner with a sign in the window that read "Breakfast Special: Ham & Eggs." The chicken suggested that they go in, but the pig adamantly refused. He explained to his companion, "Look, from you they only want a donation. From me they want a total commitment!"

We must each decide where we can authentically stand in relation to the needs of others. For most of us it generally falls somewhere between a donation that affects us only slightly and a total commitment. No one else can decide what is right for us to do or give. We can only cultivate our ability and willingness to ask and listen inside ourselves in each situation, each opportunity for giving and service in which we find ourselves — to discover what we really want to do and are able to do and also to cultivate our willingness to be true to our inner guidance.

> *No one can do everything,*
> *but everyone can do something.*
>
> — Source unknown

All True Giving Is Giving Love

Some years ago Mother Teresa was interviewed during a visit to New York. Loneliness and the feeling of being unwanted are, she stated, the most terrible kind of poverty and hunger. People in this country, she observed, are starving not primarily for bread but for love. Only what is given with love, as the expression and sharing of love, can truly remedy that profound and devastating spiritual hunger.

I remember being very affected by Mother Teresa's comments. I had always given money pretty freely to people on the street who asked for help. I come from a family that practiced *tzadakah,* a true spirit of loving charity and giving. I had learned to value generosity and the opportunity to give and had discovered early in life that in giving we do receive.

After reading Mother Teresa's observations, however, I took a closer look at the quality of my giving. I recognized that in giving change to street people, I often felt embarrassed and uncomfortable. Frequently I would avoid eye contact or any sort of human, person-to-person connection with them. I realized then that, although I might be helping in a material way, I was nevertheless contributing to the very consciousness of separation, lovelessness, and fear that underlies and gives rise to the terrible conditions of misery, poverty, horror, and pain in this world.

> *If you are not part of the solution,*
> *you are part of the problem.*
>
> — ELDRIDGE CLEAVER

I suddenly understood that whenever I gave without love, I was part of the problem. I decided that, from then on, my criterion for whether or not I would give in any particular situation would be whether or not I could give with love. If I was able to give with love, with an acknowledgment of my human and spiritual connection to this brother or sister — if I could honestly give something of myself — I would give. If, *for whatever reason,* at a particular moment I was unable to give with love, I would not give lovelessly.

Whenever that occurs, I now send a silent blessing and apology to the person, acknowledging in my mind that it is my own fear, my own disconnection from love, not anything about their worth, that is blocking my giving. I try to view these times as wake-up calls — opportunities to look at whatever is blocking my connection to love, to let go and choose once again. At such times I am grateful to my brother or sister for the gift of the chance to awaken and return to love.

The change in mind from separation and fear to unity and love is the miracle that is ours to share with the world. We are all here in this world to be *miracle workers,* through our willingness to reunite with the love in our minds and hearts and by forgiving the many times and ways we choose separation. Ken Wapnick has pointed out that the larger society in which we live is part of the classroom we have chosen for learning how to do this.

The social conditions around us mirror thoughts and beliefs we carry in our own minds and provide us with ample opportunities to explore our judgments and fears and to look at the ways we create the experience of separation from one another. We then can open our own minds and hearts to healing, accepting forgiveness for ourselves, so that we can extend healing, love, and forgiveness to others. In this process we offer the deepest level of service.

Love Increases in the Giving

Whoever has a heart full of love
always has something to give.

— POPE JOHN XXIII

When we center ourselves in love, we always have something to give. A few years ago *Newsweek* magazine reported that as the recession of the early 1990s worsened, charitable contributions decreased but volunteer activity increased. That article noted that many people who were themselves struggling with the challenge of unemployment chose to make that difficult situation in their own lives meaningful and worthwhile by volunteering their time to help others.

Dr. Karl Menninger once replied that the most important thing a person can do to maintain mental health is to "lock up your house, go across the railroad tracks, find someone in need and do something for him." Nineteenth-century poet William Wordsworth called "The best portion of a good man's life, / His little, nameless, unremembered acts, / Of kindness and of love."

What we give may or may not be material or tangible. It may or may not involve a lot of time or effort. It may be as simple as a smile, a nod, a word of kindness or encouragement. It may be a blessing or a silent wish or prayer. It is always the *content* — the love expressed in the giving — and not the form itself that makes the gift.

We are constantly teaching others and ourselves who they are, who we are, what human beings are like, what kind of world this is. As we noted earlier, we have no choice about whether or not we teach. Our only choice is *what* we will teach.

As miracle workers, we are here to be teachers of love. We will learn ourselves whatever it is we teach. If we want to learn that we can live in a world of kindness, compassion, human fellowship, and love, we must demonstrate that kind of world to others through our own thoughts, attitudes, and treatment of them. What we embody will tend to be manifest in our own experience. When we give love, no matter what the form of our giving, our own experience of love is deepened, expanded, and increased.

Service, Love, and Self-Care

Reflection and experience teach us that, if we are to be able to be caring and giving to others, we must remember to be genuinely loving and caring toward ourselves. We cannot offer what we do not have.

During the devastation of the civil war in Rwanda, I watched a news feature about an international volunteer group of doctors and nurses who were working in Zaire at a camp for Rwandan refugees. I was struck by the depth of dedication and compassion that these men and women demonstrated, as well as the matter-of-factness and practicality about helping that they embodied.

A Belgian doctor, chief physician of the team, stressed the importance of *self-care* in being able to serve others in an ongoing way. He emphasized that only by taking good enough care of themselves physically, mentally, and emotionally could the relief workers get up day after day and continue to serve. He spoke of how important it was for them to take time at the end of their day to have a good meal, relax, rest, rejuvenate and replenish themselves. Those volunteers who did not take care of themselves in that way, he observed, rarely lasted more than a week.

An American nurse added that she also took time each morning — from 5:30 to 7:00 A.M. — to reflect, write in her journal, process her feelings and experiences from the day before, and pray. She found this time of emotional clearing and spiritual centering vital to her own renewal and continued ability to help.

These sharings are compelling, in part because the circumstances of service in which these people are involved seem so overwhelming and extreme. Yet for each one of us, every day of our lives offers us countless opportunities, right where we live, to serve and be helpful. While these opportunities may be far less dramatic, they are nevertheless just as real. And the experience of the volunteers in Africa also speaks to our own capacity for service.

In the early 1980s I attended a workshop that began with some basic ground rules for the time we would be spending together. The ones that have stayed with me over the years offer solid guidelines for living a life of service as well.

1. Don't hurt yourself and don't hurt others.
2. Take care of yourself so you can take care of others.

— INSIGHT LEVEL I SEMINAR

This is simple but profoundly practical wisdom. Living our lives and caring for ourselves in such a way that we are adequately nourished and regularly replenished and renewed — physically, mentally, emotionally, and spiritually — is really a gift to the world around us. For it allows us to live our daily lives poised to help and to give.

The Far Reach of Service

In scattering the seed, scattering your "charity," your kind deeds, you are giving away in one form or another, part of your personality, and taking into yourself part of another. He who received them from you will hand them to another. And how can you tell what part you may have in the future determination of the destinies of humanity?

— FYODOR DOSTOYEVSKY

A few years ago I was hospitalized for a deep kidney infection that had led to blood poisoning. There was a shortage of space in the hospital, so I was in a room with three other people. One morning I awoke to the sound of the woman in the next bed moaning in pain. She was dying of cancer, had been bedridden for quite some time, and was often in great pain.

I was suddenly aware of the enormity and intensity of suffering that exists in the world. I felt overwhelmed and shattered by it. I wanted to shut down against that awareness, to armor my heart against the pain. At the same time I felt a deep compassion and longing to stay present and to love. I prayed for help to understand how I could keep my heart open within the awareness of that vast suffering. I knew that I needed a very different perspective, another way to see.

Over the course of the morning, I found myself very conscious of my interactions with others, especially with the nursing staff who would come into the room. I saw that in every interaction I was making a choice of what I would bring to that exchange. I could offer harshness, irritability, indifference, impatience — or I could offer kindness, friendliness, interest, humor. In this insight, I recognized the answer to my prayer. Moment by moment, in each of my interactions, I was either adding to the suffering in the world, or I was, in some small way, helping to alleviate it. There was, in fact, no neutral ground.

Sometimes it is easy for us to see the ripple effect of our own choices. But the Course assures us that the impact of our choice to offer love extends far beyond what we can ever really imagine.

A miracle is never lost. It may touch many people you have not even met, and produce undreamed of changes in situations of which you are not even aware.

—T. p. 4; T-1. I.45

Everything that comes from love, the Course says, is a miracle. And, it teaches, one miracle is not larger or greater than another. "All expressions of love are maximal" (T. p. 1; T-1.I.1:4).

We never really know how far our acts of kindness and caring will reach. This is as true and important in our personal relationships, with our families, friends, colleagues, as it is with respect to strangers or people in some kind of obvious need. Someone we treat with kindness and respect, rather than harshness or discourtesy, may treat the next person the same way — and that one the next, and that one the next. Our choices ripple out in waves that extend far beyond what we ourselves can ever see.

We cannot do great things.
We can do only small things,
with great love.

— MOTHER TERESA

We need simply to know, and remember, that no choice of love is too small, no expression of love unimportant. We can share the faith and wisdom of that man on the beach with the starfish: we can go on living our lives and doing what we can to love wherever we are, knowing in our hearts, "It made a difference to that one."

Chapter 6

Sympathetic Joy

I promise to see others' joy as my own.

You need to love all persons as yourself, esteeming them and considering them alike. What happens to another, whether it be a joy or a sorrow, happens to you.

— MEISTER ECKHART

In Buddhist teaching, the promise to see the happiness of others as our own is the promise to cultivate the state of sympathetic joy, or gladness. Creation Spirituality theologian Matthew Fox suggests that this is, in fact, the other arm of compassion. A full recognition of our oneness leads to wanting both to relieve the suffering of others and to see and celebrate their joy and happiness as our own.

Compassion and Celebration

In chapter 4, we drew a clear distinction between compassion, which is always based on love, on a recognition of kinship and equality, and pity, which is based instead on fear, on conde-

93

scension and difference. Matthew Fox offers an interesting and simple way to discern whether what we are feeling toward another is compassion or pity. He suggests that we ask ourselves this question: Would I also celebrate with this person?

> *What is of most moment in compassion is not feelings of pity but feelings of togetherness. It is this awareness of togetherness that urges us to rejoice at another's joy (celebration) and to grieve at another's sorrow. Both dimensions ... are integral to true compassion. And this, above all, separates pity from compassion for it is seldom that we would invite someone we had pity on to a common celebration.*
>
> — MATTHEW FOX, *A Spirituality Named Compassion*

True compassion flows from the recognition that we share in the fundamental cause of all suffering, namely, the belief that we are separate from God (love) and from each other. And so we also share the same need for healing and release. As we offer help and healing to another — as we teach a brother or sister that he or she is not alone, abandoned, unloved, and judged — we receive the same happy lesson ourselves. For we can offer real healing only from the love inside us, the love that is in our own minds and hearts. As we see and feel love's gentle blessing on another through us, we understand that we are not separate from that love. We receive the healing that we offer. Together we are reunited with the truth about ourselves.

The Course teaches that "to heal is to make happy" (T. p. 66; T-5.Intro.1:1). Our true nature as spirit is happiness and joy. We were born of the movement, the extension, and sharing of Divine Love, and we are continually reborn in the extension and sharing of love. And so whatever restores love to our awareness, whatever undoes our frightening and painful sense of separation, reunites us with the joy of our true nature and being.

Joy is thus a natural witness to healing, to our remembrance of who and what we really are. For who could truly open to receive even the tiniest glimpse of the limitless love God has for us — love that pours itself out to us and shares its overflowing fullness with us in every moment — and not be filled with joy? And who could feel such joy and not want to share it with everyone?

> *Joy is the most infallible sign*
> *of the presence of God.*
>
> — PIERRE TEILHARD DE CHARDIN

Healing leads to joy, and joy, whose nature is to increase by sharing itself, seeks to offer healing to others. Compassion leads to celebration, and celebration leads to compassion. Neither can exist without the other.

> *Compassion is about what I have called feelings of together-*
> *ness, suspended egos, or the "feeling of kinship with all*
> *fellow creatures." This kinship in turn urges us to celebrate*
> *our kinship. Compassion, then, is about celebration.*
>
> — MATTHEW FOX, *A Spirituality Named Compassion*

Compassion and celebration, healing and joy, are about transcending the ego, the personal and isolated sense of self that seems to make us different from one another and to keep us apart. The practice of oneness in our lives means living the understanding that we share in the pain of the ego together, we are released from the illusion of separation together, and we celebrate the truth of our deeper identity together. Just as we can learn of our oneness by offering healing to another, so can we learn of it by being willing to share in another's joy, to see another's joy as our own.

Denying Ourselves Heaven — Choosing for the Ego

> *To rejoice at another person's joy*
> *is like being in Heaven.*
>
> — MEISTER ECKHART

When we are in what the Course calls our "right mind," we naturally enjoy each other's happiness and feel enriched by others' joy. There are clearly times, however, when we are not in our right mind, when we react to other people's happiness with feelings quite different from happiness ourselves.

Mark Twain once observed that "nothing gives us quite so much pleasure as the failure of a friend," an observation that unmasks and clearly illustrates the ego's basic nature. Conversely, it seems that sometimes nothing elicits quite so much pain in us as someone else's happiness or good fortune. We may find ourselves reacting to another's happiness and joy with feelings of envy or jealousy, loss or emptiness, irritation, resentment, even outright hostility.

In order to understand and forgive these reactions and release ourselves from the guilt they generate in us, we need to look more closely at the dynamics of the ego, the separated self — especially at the dynamics of the belief in lack, scarcity, and deprivation.

The Belief in Scarcity and Deprivation

The Course teaches that the ego is simply a part of our belief about ourselves. Specifically it is the belief that we have separated ourselves from God and the rest of creation. It is the denial that we are one with our Creator and that we share fully in the abundance of all creation. We see ourselves as less than whole, full of needs that we must try to satisfy to be complete. This belief is described in the Course as the *scarcity principle* and is basic to the entire ego thought system.

Ken Wapnick defines the scarcity principle this way:

scarcity principle: *an aspect of guilt; the belief that we are empty and incomplete, lacking what we need; this leads to our seeking idols or special relationships to fill the scarcity we experience within ourselves; often associated with feelings of deprivation, wherein we believe others are depriving*

us of the peace which in reality we have taken from ourselves;
contrasted with God's principle of abundance

— KENNETH WAPNICK,
Glossary-Index for A Course in Miracles

The Course goes on say that "the ego literally lives by comparisons" (T. p. 52; T-4.II.7:1) — that it attempts to "prove" its own reality and existence by continually evaluating itself in relation to other egos.

The ego sets up idols and defines them as necessary to our happiness and well-being. It then compares itself with other egos with respect to these idols, judging who has and who doesn't have, who has more and who has less. The ego is not really concerned with what the particular idol is or with who is lacking it. As long as *someone* appears to be lacking *something* that matters, then separation, difference, and the ego must be real.

We said earlier that joy is a witness to healing, to the undoing of separation and the restoration of love to our awareness. The New Testament teaches that "the fruit of the spirit is joy." Joy and happiness bear witness to our true identity as spirit, forever one with the fullness and abundance of God. Thus they represent a "threat" to the ego, because if spirit is real the ego is not. The Course teaches that ego always responds to a perceived threat with attack, because to the ego attack is safety and salvation.

The ego will attack joy wherever it sees it, twisting our perception so that the witness to abundance becomes instead a witness for lack. When we are happy, the ego will often attack us with thoughts and feelings of unworthiness, guilt, worry, and so on. If we see someone else happy, the ego will focus on whatever he or she seems to have that we do not have and use that to reinforce our own sense of lack. This gives rise to feelings of envy, loss, sadness, depression. Projecting the cause of our sense of lack outside of us, we feel deprived. We then feel resentful and angry toward whomever we see as depriving us.

Identified with the ego, we will see others as separate from us, different from us, in competition with us, having what we lack or lacking what we have. We cannot possibly respond with happiness to another's happiness or see another's joy as our own when we are viewing the world through the ego's eyes. That is simply the nature of the ego.

A Personal Experience of Healing

Several years ago, before I was a student of the Course, I found myself tormented by feelings of envy. Some close friends of mine were reaping great success at the time, professionally and financially, and were enjoying the increased freedom this afforded them. I was struggling at the time, having recently made a career change, and found myself resentful about not having the same level of freedom, security, and abundance. I became consumed by painful feelings of envy and deprivation.

To make things even worse, I felt ugly inside for feeling this way. These were friends I dearly loved. I wanted to feel happy for them. Instead I felt bitter, deprived, and diminished somehow by their success. Intellectually I knew better. I understood that their success did not in any real way deprive or limit me. But that intellectual understanding didn't help. In fact, it seemed only to deepen my feelings of shame and guilt.

I felt as though I were living in hell. I tried everything I could think of to get rid of my feelings of bitterness and envy. I pulled out every trick and technique in my psychological grab-bag, acquired through years of professional training and personal therapy. Nothing worked. My despair deepened as I realized how central a place envy had occupied at times in certain other friendships as well. Finally, one morning, I sat on the floor in my bedroom and said, to no one in particular, "I give up."

In retrospect, it was a moment of true surrender. At the time, it did not feel like a choice. I knew that I did not want to feel the way I was feeling. I knew that the problem was not outside of me, but inside. And I knew that there was nothing I knew how to do to make it better. I don't remember if I consciously prayed, but something inside me had quietly said, "Help!"

Over the next few days and weeks, I gradually became aware that my feelings of envy seemed to be dissolving. It felt as if an enormous emotional burden I'd been carrying had been somehow lifted from me. The experience was one of grace. I felt a profound sense of both release and gratitude.

I found that I began naturally to feel happy for my friends' successes and able to share their happiness. And, looking back, I realize that I also felt a sense of reconciliation with myself — as if I had come home somehow to a truer self in me.

Comparing — The Block to Sympathetic Joy

Comparison must be an ego device,
for love makes none.

—T. p. 466; T-24.II.1:1

The major block to our experiencing sympathetic joy is our habit of comparing ourselves to others. The experience of jealousy or envy, such as I experienced in relation to my friends, obviously involves a process of making comparisons. We look at what someone else has, or is, and see ourselves as lacking that. And we define whatever that is as being somehow essential to our own happiness, fulfillment, and well-being.

We can also get caught in making comparisons with our own past. We may look back with nostalgia on a time when we "had" something we've now "lost" — for instance, a job, a relationship, the physical vitality of youth, money, a lack of responsibilities, a time in the spotlight. If we believe that what we no longer have is essential to our feelings of self-esteem and happiness, we will feel deprived and lacking in relation to our former selves.

Teacher and healer Brugh Joy, author of *Joy's Way,* has said that one of the keys to true happiness is to *stop comparing.* After the experience I described earlier, I began to notice just how much, how habitually, I compared myself to other people. It seemed I did it all the time.

What I discovered as I began to observe more closely this habit of comparing is that it *always* led to inner pain. If I compared my-self unfavorably to someone else, I would feel bad about myself — deficient, inadequate, unworthy, unlovable, and so on. But even when I compared myself favorably with others — which really meant that I saw myself as somehow better, more worthy, or more lovable than they — I realized that on some level I still felt bad. Deep down I realized that I was making myself feel good at their expense. By judging them as "less than," by diminishing their value and worth in my perception, it seemed that I could increase my own. It occurred to me that this was not a very kind or lov-ing thing to do to people. And so I discovered that comparing is always a losing game, whether or not I seemed to win or lose in the comparison.

The function of comparing is to make different, to separate and divide. Comparing ourselves with others serves to increase our ex-perience of separation from them. This is inevitably painful, for it replicates and deepens our experience of separation from God and from our own true self.

Comparing ourselves with others always obscures our knowing of ourselves and others as whole and complete. For comparing al-ways involves distortion and fragmentation. We select out limited pieces of someone's life situation or personality to be compared to our own, and then we look at these without reference or concern for the whole picture, the totality of the other or ourselves. Com-parison focuses exclusively on what reinforces our experience of lack or deprivation, or on what makes us seem "better" or "more worthy" than someone else. Our perceptions of both ourselves and the other person are partial, incomplete, and thus inevitably distorted.

Honoring Our Uniqueness

Everybody is unique.
Compare not yourself with anybody else
Lest you spoil God's curriculum.

— THE BAAL SHEM TOV

By distorting our perception of ourselves through comparing ourselves to others, we miss discovering the deeper beauty and joy of who we really are and what our unique lives are about. By focusing on things external to ourselves that we think would bring us happiness — or on personality qualities we think we need in order to acquire those external things — we delay discovering that happiness and fulfillment already lie within us, waiting to be released into expression.

Every one of us has a unique and precious part to play in the plan of creation. No one's part is any more or less important than anyone else's, just as in a symphony no note is more or less important than another to the whole, or in a tapestry no single thread is of greater or lesser value than any other. Each one is an integral part of the totality, each perfect in its place, each of equal value and essential to the whole creation.

Our true happiness in life comes as we understand, appreciate, and say yes more and more deeply to our right relationship and meaningful place in the whole of things. Whatever our place, only we can fill it. Whatever our contribution, only we can make it. Whatever our gifts, only we can offer them.

We cannot discover what we have to offer while we are busy comparing ourselves to others. Our part in the plan in not someone else's, nor is another's part our own. We each have lessons to learn and teach for which our own lives are the perfectly designed classroom. No one else's life is better suited to our real needs, which our deeper wisdom recognizes and understands and our ego has no idea of. We need to be willing to learn our own lessons and accept that others are learning theirs. We are each on our own path, which we must follow. Our own path will lead us home.

As we begin to recognize and honor the uniqueness of our particular path of learning and healing, we also begin to realize that there is a deeper commonality we share. Just as we all long to be released from suffering, we all long to experience happiness. The success and happiness of others on their journeys can teach us that success and happiness are possible for us as well. We wish them well, as we wish ourselves well. Sympathetic joy is born in our hearts.

Practicing Sympathetic Joy

It is important that we not use this description of the ego's dynamics to feel guilty about the times we compare ourselves to other people or respond to others' happiness with feelings of envy, sadness, deprivation, or anger. That only perpetuates the ego system and the deep suffering it entails. If we are to cultivate sympathetic joy we need simply to recognize that whenever we respond without joy to another's joy we have gotten caught up in the ego — and to remember that our own need then is to come gently back to love.

The promise to see others' joy as our own will tend to bring to the surface all the ways our ego blocks our natural inclination and ability to do that. In a meditation practice we learn to notice our wandering thoughts and bring them gently back to a mantra, to the breath, to the Name of God, to the day's Workbook lesson. In the same way we can learn to notice the manifestations of our ego and bring them gently back to the love in our hearts, to the light of forgiveness in our minds that shines them away.

As we continue to offer the ego to love — interweaving the practice of sympathetic joy with the practice of loving kindness and compassion toward ourselves — we reunite with the truth in us. Centered in that truth, we cannot help but celebrate and share the joy that reflects Heaven here on earth.

Chapter 7

Appreciation and Gratitude: The Way of a Thankful Heart

*God has two dwellings: one in heaven,
the other in a thankful heart.*

— Izaak Walton

*If I do not feel a sense of joy in God's creation, if I forget
to offer the world back to God with thankfulness, I have ad-
vanced very little upon the Way. I have not yet learnt to be
truly human. For it is only in thanksgiving that I can become
myself.*

— St. John of Kronstadt

Among the most important spiritual practices we can engage in —
especially if we are to develop our capacity for sympathetic joy,
to be glad for the success and happiness of others — are those of
gratitude and thankfulness. As we practice and develop these attitudes of heart and mind, life becomes increasingly rich and full,
miraculous and satisfying. And we become more and more aware
of God's presence in our lives.

*Gratitude to God becomes the way in which He is remem-
bered, for love cannot be far behind a grateful heart and*

thankful mind. God enters easily, for these are the true conditions for your homecoming.

—M. p. 55; M-23.4:6–7

Especially important to the development of gratitude is cultivating a basic attitude of *appreciation* toward life.

Appreciating Being Alive

*Normal day, let me be aware
of the treasure that you are.*

— MARY JEAN IRION

The power and importance of appreciating life were beautifully depicted a few years ago in the film *Awakenings*. The film was based on the true story of Dr. Oliver Sachs, a neurologist who spent part of his early career working in a chronic care hospital with patients suffering from a severe post-encephalitic disorder. The condition had rendered these people catatonic and unresponsive to the world.

In the film the doctor—a socially awkward and insecure young man whose work previously had been confined to laboratory research — discovers signs of responsiveness in these patients. He and his staff begin searching intensely for ways of reaching and establishing a connection with them. They conclude that, indeed, "somebody is at home in there."

Confronting quite a bit of skepticism, conservatism, and reluctance on the part of the medical administration of the hospital, the doctor persists and gets permission to administer an experimental drug to one of the patients. The man undergoes a miraculous "awakening." As if he had literally been somewhere else for thirty years, suddenly he is *back* — present as a living, moving, communicating, interacting, *fully alive* human being. The same medication is given to all the other patients suffering from the same disorder, with the same results.

The film beautifully and poignantly depicts the tremendous joy these reawakened people experience in the *simple things* we so often take for granted — walking, talking, looking out a window, meeting people, dancing, playing music, combing our hair, offering a word of hope or solace to another human being, having and being a friend.

The medication eventually caused severe side effects and had to be discontinued. The patients all returned to their isolated, unresponsive, "somewhere else" state of existence. For that one summer, though, they had sounded a clear and unmistakable "wake up" call to the young doctor and all the other "normal" people around them:

> *Live fully — Celebrate life!*
> *Don't take anything for granted!*
> *Participate — Get involved!*
> *Make the most of every moment!*
> *Be alive!!!*

Appreciation and Awareness

> *When you really fill your days*
> *with love and appreciation,*
> *you will know the true meaning of life.*
>
> — EILEEN CADDY

Life is filled with gifts and blessings, offered to us freely and graciously, waiting to surprise and delight us. One of my favorite descriptions of the abundance that is everywhere around us comes from Annie Dillard's *Pilgrim at Tinker Creek.*

> *When I was six or seven years old, growing up in Pittsburgh,*
> *I used to take a precious penny of my own and hide it for*
> *someone else to find. I was greatly excited...at the thought*

*of the first lucky passerby who would receive in this way,
regardless of merit, a free gift from the universe....*

    *I've been thinking about seeing. There are lots of things
to see, unwrapped gifts and free surprises. The world is
fairly studded and strewn with pennies cast broadside from
a generous hand.*

         — Annie Dillard, *Pilgrim at Tinker Creek*

The first step toward gratitude and appreciation is awareness.
We need to open our eyes, look around us, and see what is there.
To be fully alive is to be alert, *awake*. To appreciate life we need
to be attentive, receptive, and present in and to this moment. We
can be awake and alive only *now*.

What generally separates us from the present moment — and
from being fully alive — is getting caught up in our ego thoughts,
our conditioned and habitual ways of thinking and reacting. We
rehash the past and rehearse the future. In our minds we are often
somewhere else in space or time.

Living much of our time in a fantasy world of worries, fears,
regrets, hopes, plans, and "what-if's," we lose touch with the
present moment, with ourselves, with the only place we can ever
find blessing, joy, and peace.

    Heaven is here. There is nowhere else.
    Heaven is now. There is no other time.

         —M. p. 58; M-24.6:4–7

To return to the experience of peace, abundance of blessing, and
happiness that reflects Heaven now and here, we need to cultivate
the ability to recognize when we have gotten caught up in the dis-
traction and chatter of our ego thoughts and substituted them for
reality. We need to learn to step back from these thoughts, notice
them, and gently return our awareness to the present.

As we noted in chapter 1, the state of awareness in and to the
present moment is called *mindfulness*. Living mindfully opens the
way for opening our hearts to appreciation.

Machine thinking is the opposite of mindfulness. If we're really engaged in mindfulness while walking along the path to the village, then we will consider the act of each step we take as an infinite wonder, and a joy will open our hearts like a flower, enabling us to enter the world of reality.

— THICH NHAT HANH, *The Miracle of Mindfulness*

Awareness and appreciation are inseparable. Appreciation follows naturally from awareness, from being fully awake to and present in the moment. What we are fully present with, we can *understand* — not with our intellects alone, but with a deeper knowing and recognition of the heart. What we understand with our hearts, we can truly appreciate. And what we fully appreciate, we discover that we love.

Understanding brings appreciation
and appreciation brings love.

—T. p. 115; T-7.VI.6:6

Appreciation undoes our sense of separation and distance, for what we appreciate we open our hearts to and embrace as a part of ourselves. As we offer appreciation, our own sense of fullness is increased.

Giving and Receiving—Appreciation and Increase

By giving you receive. But to receive is to accept, not to get. It is impossible not to have, but it is possible not to know you have.

—T. p. 154; T-9.II.11:4–6

A friend of mine once described appreciation as being like a *hug*—an act in which you both *give and receive* at the same time. Appreciation is a wonderful demonstration of the teaching that "to give and to receive are one in truth" (W. p. 191; W-Pt.I.108).

What we appreciate we give value to, by recognizing and acknowledging its worth. We offer it blessing, love, and gratitude.
As we give appreciation, we *experience and accept more fully*
whatever it is that we appreciate. We are more aware of its presence in our lives, of the gift it is and the blessing it offers us. We
more fully *receive* that which we appreciate.

We have been taught that as we sow, so shall we reap. Sowing
seeds of appreciation yields a rich and abundant harvest of blessings. The more we actively appreciate life, the more, it seems, there
is to appreciate.

> *Divine Love is so immensely great! Great is its overflow, for
> Divine Love is never still. Always ceaselessly and tirelessly
> it pours itself out so that the small vessel which is ourselves
> might be filled to the brim and also overflow.*
>
> — MECHTILD OF MAGDEBURG

Life is, indeed, "fairly studded and strewn" with gifts, poured
out to us generously and continuously. This is true even at those
times when the outer conditions of our lives may not be especially
to our liking. Blessings abound, but often we do not have the eyes
to see what is really there.

Obstacles to Blessing: Fault-Finding

> *A thankful person is thankful
> under all circumstances.
> A complaining soul complains
> even if he lives in paradise.*
>
> — BAHA'U'LLAH

To appreciate something is to focus on its worth, to value it. If
an investment appreciates, it increases in value. In the same way,
if an investment depreciates, it decreases in value and diminishes
in worth.

There are two primary ways in which we depreciate things and people in our lives, two major obstacles to receiving and experiencing life's blessings. The first of these is *fault-finding*. One of the principles of attitudinal healing, developed by Gerald Jampolsky and elaborated by Susan Trout, is that *we can be either love-finders or fault-finders*. And we will *always* find what we are looking for.

Fault-finding focuses on what is wrong, what is lacking, what "ought" to be different. It may take the form of overt criticism, judgment, attack, or put-down. Or it may take the more subtle forms of complaining or worrying.

In this frame of mind, we feel short-changed and deprived, envious of or bitter toward others who seem to have what we believe we lack. Instead of feeling supported by and connected to life, we feel isolated, cut off, and separate. The goodness, fullness, and joy of life seem to be happening somewhere else, to someone else.

We harvest what we cultivate. The more we focus on finding fault and complaining, the more we can find to complain about. The more we focus on what we think is missing in our lives, the more we miss what is *present*.

It is always possible to be thankful for what is given rather than to complain about what is not given. One or the other becomes a habit of life.

— ELISABETH ELLIOT

Fault-finding and complaining become habits. We engage in them so automatically that we may not even realize how much of our time they occupy, how much of our mental and emotional energy they consume.

Several years ago I heard a talk by a lively and delightful Unity minister who shared the following lesson about fault-finding in her own spiritual development. Many years earlier she had been in her pastor's office one Sunday morning after the worship service, complaining about how other members of the congregation just couldn't seem to do even the simplest tasks for the church properly. After she had gone on this way for quite some time, her minister told her, gently but quite firmly:

My dear, for you right now, the highest metaphysical principle in the entire universe is: Don't Bitch!

Although she was quite certain at the time that — for once — he must be wrong, she nevertheless had enough respect for this man who had been her mentor to take his advice seriously. She decided that for one month she would not complain about or find fault with anyone or anything. She marked the days off, one by one, on her calendar.

To her amazement, this very talkative woman — who was, by her own report, *never* at a loss for words — discovered that for the first week or so she had *nothing at all to say!* Fault-finding and complaining had permeated her entire perception and conversation. Without that focus, she felt disoriented, her mind empty and blank. But then something wonderful began to happen. The vacuum that was left by not complaining began to be filled by the presence of the Holy Spirit, by gentleness, inspiration and love.

What you leave as vacant God will fill.

—T. p. 532; T-27.III.4:3

Loving thoughts, perceptions, and comments began to occur to her spontaneously and naturally. And her experience of love and well-being in life increased dramatically.

We can be fault-finders or love-finders — but not both. Each purpose blocks the other from our sight. Whichever we choose will determine the quality of our experience of life. We can experience deprivation or we can experience abundance of blessing — in the very same outer circumstances. It is our choice to make. Which do you prefer?

Obstacles to Blessing: Taking Things for Granted

A less obvious, and thus more insidious, obstacle to the experience of appreciation and blessing in our lives is taking what we have for granted. As the patients in the film *Awakenings* demonstrated so clearly, there are many, many simple things in our lives that we would *miss terribly* if we couldn't do or have them. Yet generally we take them for granted rather than truly appreciate them.

When we take things or people for granted, we cut ourselves off from the richness of blessing we could experience right now. We go through life like sleepwalkers, unaware of life's continuous outpouring of gifts. We need to wake up to the moment — to what is here right now that we can open our hearts to, appreciate, enjoy, and receive more fully.

Being a love-finder means opening our eyes and our hearts, looking around us and really seeing what's here. To be fully alive is not to seek the extraordinary, but to be awake to the blessing, the miracle, within the ordinary.

> *Every morning, when we wake up, we have twenty-four brand new hours to live. What a precious gift! We have the capacity to live in a way that these twenty-four hours will bring peace, joy and happiness to ourselves and others.... We don't have to travel far to enjoy the blue sky. We don't have to leave our city or even our neighborhood to enjoy the eyes of a beautiful child.... We can smile, breathe, walk, and eat our meals in a way that allows us to be in touch with the abundance of happiness that is available.... Every breath we take, every step we make, can be filled with peace, joy, and serenity. We need only to be awake, alive in the present moment.*
>
> — THICH NHAT HANH, *Peace Is Every Step*

Deciding to cultivate an attitude of appreciation and gratitude is a powerful spiritual practice. We can wake up to the present moment and open ourselves to receive all that we have to be thankful for. We can live in the fullness of life and come to know ourselves as heirs and recipients of the Kingdom that is truly at hand, that is ever being given.

Appreciating Difficulty

Some people wish for a life of no problems, but I would never wish such a life for any of you. What I wish for you is the great inner strength to solve your problems meaningfully and grow. Problems are learning and growing experiences. A life without problems would be a barren existence, without the opportunity for spiritual growth.

— PEACE PILGRIM, *Her Life and Work in Her Own Words*

The greatest challenge in working with gratitude and appreciation as a spiritual practice comes in confronting life's problems and difficulties. Problems and adversity are part of every human life. How we respond to these experiences will largely determine what they turn out to be in our lives: tragedies and defeats, or gateways to blessing, to greater fullness of life and love.

Shakespeare wrote, "Sweet are the uses of adversity, / Which, like the toad, ugly and venomous, / Wears yet a precious jewel in his head." Every situation and experience in our lives contains a gift, a precious jewel of blessing for us. Yet, as Polly Berends points out in her book *Coming to Life,* we may be strongly tempted to reject the gift unopened because we so dislike the wrapping in which it arrives.

In Japanese, the word for "thank you" is *arigato,* which means, literally, "hardship exists." There is spiritual wisdom and maturity in recognizing the opportunity for blessings that comes in the guise of our problems.

There was a time when I thought it was a nuisance to be confronted with a problem. I tried to get rid of it. I tried to get somebody else to solve it for me. But that was a long

*time ago. It was a great day in my life when I discovered the
wonderful purpose of problems.*

— PEACE PILGRIM, *Her Life and Work in Her Own Words*

Problems offer us a chance to grow, to discover inner strengths
and resources, to develop new skills and abilities. Each one provides an opportunity to deepen our faith and our relationship
with God's Spirit within us, to practice forgiveness and receive its
healing gifts. Each one challenges us to let go of outmoded and
unproductive ways of thinking and doing things, to reassess and
clarify our values, to change our course or recommit ourselves in
a deeper fashion to a path we have chosen.

Often in hindsight we recognize the blessing that was contained
in a problem or difficulty that we experienced and overcame. We
can begin to bring this awareness to bear on challenges we are
currently facing, and perhaps move through them more gracefully, with less fear and distress. In Buddhist teaching this is
referred to as "making our difficulties into our path." With this
understanding and attitude, all of life befriends us, all of life
enriches us.

*The seeds of wisdom, peace, and wholeness are within each
of our difficulties. Our awakening is possible in every activity. At first we may sense this truth only tentatively. With
practice it becomes living reality. Our spiritual life can open a
dimension of our being where each person we meet can teach
us like the Buddha and whatever we touch becomes gold. To
do this we must make our difficulties the place of our practice. Then our life becomes not a struggle with success and
failure but a dance of the heart. It is up to us.*

— JACK KORNFIELD, *A Path with Heart*

We will explore the process of opening to the blessings that lie
within our difficulties in more depth in Chapter 9.

Giving Thanks

If the only prayer you ever say
in your whole life is "thank you,"
that would suffice.

— MEISTER ECKHART

Thankfulness and gratitude are natural outcomes of cultivating appreciation for life. "Thank you" flows forth naturally from the heart that is open to receive and filled to overflowing. As we give thanks, our hearts expand, our capacity to receive expands, and we are filled with ever-increasing blessings to extend and share.

Taking stock of our blessings, crystallizing and expressing all that we are thankful for in our lives, is a deeply enriching and empowering process. The practice of acknowledgment and of giving thanks centers us, establishes us in right relationship with life and our Source, and opens the way for greater expression of life to flow through us to bless us, those we love, and all the world around us.

Chapter 8

Nonattachment and Equanimity

*I promise to learn the way of nonattachment
and equanimity.*

*Learn to be quiet in the midst of turmoil,
for quietness is the end of strife
and this is the journey to peace.*

—T. p. 204; T-12.II.5:5

*Remember, no human condition is ever permanent.
Then you will not be overjoyed in good fortune
nor too sorrowful in misfortune.*

— SOCRATES

When I first read the four promises in the gatha offered by Thich Nhat Hanh for beginning to eat, I found it interesting that the final one is phrased specifically in terms of *learning*. The way of nonattachment is completely foreign to the normal thinking of the world, and the ego defends strongly against it. Learning the way of nonattachment is essentially the process of learning to *disidentify* with the ego, of learning that the ego is not who or what we are.

The Nature of Attachment —
The Belief in Specialness

Your mission is very simple.
You are asked to live so as to demonstrate
that you are not an ego....

—T. p. 62; T-4.VI.6:2–3

The fundamental teachings of the Buddha are summarized in what are called the Four Noble Truths. The first of these is that the nature of our existence here is suffering. The second is that the cause of suffering is desire, or attachment. The third noble truth is that escape from suffering is possible. The fourth states that suffering can be escaped by following the Eightfold Path, the practices outlined by the Buddha for attaining enlightenment. Expressed more inclusively, the fourth noble truth is that suffering can be escaped by following a spiritual path that truly prepares our minds to awaken.

In Buddhist teaching, desire or attachment is also described as *ignorance* — ignorance of the workings of mind, ignorance of the empty or illusory nature of the phenomenal world, ignorance of our own true nature and the reality of oneness. In the context of the Course, the fundamental attachment that causes all of our suffering is our attachment to the belief in separation, to the "reality" of the ego, to our identity as a separate, individual self.

This self is inherently *egocentric*. We literally perceive, define, and react to everything in relation to this self — to what we believe we are, what we believe we need, what we believe will make us happy and secure and safe. This self is grounded in what the Course refers to as our belief in *specialness*. Specialness *is* egocentrism.

Specialness is the belief, conscious or unconscious, overt or covert, that what I want or think I need is most important, that the world should somehow revolve around me. It is based on the belief that it is possible to want something apart from and opposed to the Will of God. The Course teaches that God loves everyone equally because God loves everyone totally. Specialness wants to be loved *more,* to receive special favor or special treatment.

By denying the perfect equality of creation, the goal of specialness also denies the totality of love. Thus it opens a space in our minds for fear to enter — for competition, conflict, attack, defense, and guilt, for all the "drama" that comprises the story line of our lives and substitutes for the peace of God. It is this dynamic that literally gives rise to and maintains the dream of separation.

In the substitution of the dream for our awareness of reality, it makes no difference who plays which role in the drama — who appears to be victim and who appears to be victimizer, who appears to attack and who appears to defend. By perceiving conflict, competition, and attack, by giving events that definition in our minds, we reinforce the ego and deny peace.

> *You add as much strife to the world*
> *when you take offense*
> *as when you give it.*
>
> — KEN KEYES, JR.

To understand the dynamics of specialness, it is important to understand that the belief in specialness is not necessarily manifest in what the world would call high self-esteem. People with so-called low self-esteem also define their world in self-referential fashion. Most simply, specialness means that each of us views ourselves as the "hero" — the central figure — of our own story. From this egocentric point of view, we inevitably see everyone else on some level as secondary characters, who really "ought" to serve the function we have assigned to them in order to fulfill our happiness and well-being as we have defined them.

> *When you are angry, is it not because someone has failed to fill the function you allotted him? And does not this become the "reason" your attack is justified? The dreams you think you like are those in which the functions you have given have been filled; the needs which you ascribe to you*

*are met ... each (dream) represents some function that you
have assigned; some goal which an event, or body, or thing
should represent, and should achieve for you. If it succeeds
you think you like the dream. If it should fail you think the
dream is sad.*

                                        —T. p. 569; T-29.VI.4:1–3, 8–10

We react to events and to other people based on whether we see
them as upholding or challenging our specialness. Meanwhile they
are doing the same. Because specialness is based on *inequality* —
one has more by another having less — specialness is inherently
subject and vulnerable to competition, threat, and attack.

Specialness is the basic content of all our dreams of fear. Identifying with our specialness, with its vulnerability to attack and
hurt, keeps the seeming reality of the dream in place. All of the
world's apparent assaults on our specialness serve to reinforce its
reality in our minds and to hide the greater truth of what we are
from our awareness. The Course describes clearly the subjective
experience of being attached to, or identified with, our specialness.

*It is not you who are so vulnerable and open to attack that
just a word, a little whisper that you do not like, a circumstance that suits you not, or an event that you did not
anticipate upsets your world, and hurls it into chaos. Truth
is not frail. Illusions leave it perfectly unmoved and undisturbed. But specialness is not the truth in you. It can be
thrown off balance by anything. What rests on nothing can
never be stable. However large and overblown it seems to be,
it still must rock and turn and whirl about with every breeze.*

                                        —T. p. 470; T-24. III.3

It is our attachment to specialness, to the ego, that is our
greatest block to awakening to our true Self. Our healing process, which prepares us for this awakening, is thus a process of
gradually letting go of our attachment to specialness, of our identification with the ego. Little by little, we learn to recognize and

give up our attachment to all the symbols of specialness we have made. We learn the way of nonattachment.

Nonattachment, Acceptance, and Choice

Dreams are perceptual temper tantrums,
in which you literally scream, "I want it thus!"

— T. p. 350; T-18.II.4:1

The dream of specialness was born of our nonacceptance, or rejection, of the reality of God's equal and total love for all creation as one. Our attachment to specialness is reinforced each time we refuse to accept what is in our lives at this moment and argue that things should be different than they are. We repeat in microcosm the original mistake that the Course calls the authority problem, the idea that we know better than God what reality ought to be and the insane notion that we could design it better than God has.

The ego teaches us that our peace of mind, happiness, and sense of well-being are all determined by something outside of us. The more preoccupied we become with externals, the more power we give them and the more disempowered we feel. Focusing on what we see as wrong with the circumstances of the moment distracts us from acknowledging the decision-making power of our own mind to choose peace instead of turmoil and love instead of fear. This is what keeps the entire ego thought system intact. By maintaining a denial that the peace and love of God already exist as alternatives within our own mind, we maintain our belief that we are separate from peace and love.

Learning the way of nonattachment involves reclaiming the power of our mind to choose our attitude and perception at any moment, regardless of the circumstances in which we find ourselves. It means accepting that we can always choose peace, we can always choose love, no matter how distressing the outer situation may objectively appear. Jesus clearly demonstrated the power of this choice. Many other human beings throughout history have also taught by living example that this power and ability are forever within us.

> *We who lived in concentration camps can remember the men who walked through the huts comforting others, giving away their last piece of bread. They may have been few in number, but they offer sufficient proof that everything can be taken away from a man but one thing: the last of human freedoms — to choose one's attitude in any given set of circumstances, to choose one's own way.*
>
> — VIKTOR E. FRANKL, *Man's Search for Meaning*

Most of us do not need to learn and teach this lesson under such extreme outer conditions. We can begin with the many little insults, slights, or challenges to our specialness, to our ego, that occur each day. There will always be things in our lives that are not to our ego's liking. We can start there to learn that those things cannot rob us of peace if we make an inner choice of peace, if we practice forgiveness instead of judgment and attack.

Every situation we find ourselves in can teach us of our true freedom and power as a child of God. We can learn progressively to be still and centered even in the midst of the storms that are so much a part of life in this world. And as we do, we become true teachers of peace.

Nonattachment and the Undoing of Specialness

All judgments the ego makes are based on specialness. We believe we like or love those things, people, situations, or events that seem to protect, reinforce, and uphold our specialness. We dislike or even hate those things, people, situations, or events that seem to challenge, threaten, or undermine it. Since life here is full of such experiences, to the extent that we are identified with the ego, identified with specialness, a lasting sense of inner peace or equanimity must elude us. Peace comes to us as we recognize and relinquish our attachment to the ego and its symbols.

The ego sees the purpose of the world as being to uphold this specialness and the entire thought system of separation that it is built upon and reinforces. The Holy Spirit, the Course teaches, sees a very different purpose for the world. To the Holy Spirit the world is a classroom in which specialness and separation can be undone and the remembrance of love can dawn again in our awareness. This is what the Course means by healing. And this healing, the Course teaches, is the only purpose the world has, the only value it can offer.

> *Forget not that the healing of God's Son is all the world is for. That is the only purpose the Holy Spirit sees in it, and thus the only one it has. Until you see the healing of the Son as all you wish to be accomplished by the world, by time, and by all appearances, you will not know the Father nor yourself.*
>
> —T. p. 476; T-24.VI.4:1–3

Suffering is built into the very fabric and foundation of the ego's world because the world of separation was made to oppose the eternal joy, abundance, and life of God's creation. We can be released from this suffering as we are willing to stop looking to the world to give us what it cannot give, the gifts of God: perfect safety, perfect peace, perfect happiness, perfect love.

The Course teaches that these gifts are already within us, within our own hearts and minds. As we choose to give them to the world, to look at the world through eyes of love rather than judgment, we recognize and receive them as our own. The fear, insecurity, and pain inherent in specialness, separate interests, competition, and inequality give way to a joyful awareness that all creation shares as one in love that knows no condition or limit.

This love, the love of God, is ever present and ever extending. We can turn away from it in our minds, but it can never abandon or withhold itself from us. Listening to and identifying with the ego can hide the gifts of God from our awareness — but cannot destroy them. Love is within us, peace is within us, and we can choose at any moment to return. The power of our return lies within us, within our choice, and not in anything in or of the world.

> *And turn you to the stately calm within where in holy stillness dwells the living God you never left, and Who never left you.*
>
> —T. p. 348; T-18. I.8:2

The Process of Changing Our Minds

The Course teaches that we begin to relinquish the ego by being willing to look at the ego and call into question its perceptions, judgments, and interpretations. By "loosening" our attachment to the ego's point of view, by recognizing that there might be another way, a better way, of looking at a situation, we open to the possibility of a real change. The Holy Spirit, the deeper wisdom of our heart, would offer us a very different perception and interpretation of the situation, one that offers us a lesson of healing and peace.

The two interpretations of any situation — that of the ego and that of the Holy Spirit — are completely different from each other in every respect. The ego's version is built upon images of specialness, conflict, guilt, victimization, and fear, and reinforces their seeming reality in our minds. The Holy Spirit's perception unmasks all those frightening images and leads us gently back to an awareness of love.

Our *only* choice, the Course insists, is between these two alternatives. Whenever we are upset, fearful, or not at peace about a situation, we have already interpreted with our ego. We "ask for" the Holy Spirit's interpretation instead by deciding that we do not want the one we made, by being willing to be wrong, and by recognizing that we do not know what the situation means or how to look at it. By leaving an open space in our minds, love's perception enters our awareness. We recognize it by the peace it brings.

Love's perception is already and always present in our minds, in what the Course calls our "right mind." When we are fearful, judgmental, caught up in defending our specialness, we are not in our right mind. As we acknowledge this and are willing to ask for help to look at things differently, the situation that seemed the source of our pain is transformed into a lesson of healing and joy — whether or not the situation changes in an outer sense.

The Lesson God Would Have Us Learn — a Personal Example

This is the lesson God would have you learn:
There is a way to look on everything
that lets it be to you another step to Him.

—W. p. 359; W-Pt.I.193.13:1

There is nothing we can go through in this world that cannot be part of our healing into a fuller awareness of love. There is no experience that cannot serve our healing into joy. There is nothing that cannot be used by the Teacher of peace to restore us to deeper and more lasting peace.

All things work together for good.
There are no exceptions
except in the ego's judgment.

—T. p. 59; T-4.V.1:1–2

A few years ago I had a clear opportunity to work very directly with this idea. The situation involved was fairly minor in an "objective," worldly sense and, perhaps for that reason, allowed me to experience in a short span of time a powerful lesson in healing and love.

My colleague Jon Mundy and I were traveling by train to Charlottesville, Virginia, where we were to present a workshop the following day. The trip ordinarily takes about seven hours, and we were enjoying the time just to read and relax. Between Baltimore and Washington, D.C., however, the train lost all engine power. We had to wait over an hour for another engine to be sent from Washington to pull us the rest of the way into the Washington station.

Once the train was back underway, there continued to be additional problems and delays. The train was running further and further behind schedule, and the hour was getting late. The later it got, the more frayed everyone's nerves were becoming. I could feel myself becoming increasingly irritable and agitated and could sense that same kind of energy throughout the whole car. It was being expressed most noticeably by a mother traveling alone with her young son. The child was very active and talkative. The mother was clearly reaching the limits of her frustration and tolerance with him and began telling him angrily to shut up and go to sleep. He had no interest at all in doing either.

My own sense of agitation escalated as I watched their interaction. The workshop we were giving the next day was on the meaning and nature of service, and I found myself wanting to be of help somehow in the situation. It was very apparent to me, though, that I could be of no use to anyone in the frame of mind I was in.

I closed my eyes and began repeating over and over the first line of the Prayer of St. Francis: "Lord, make me an instrument of Your peace." I prayed for healing of my own mind so that I *could* extend peace to others. Finally I felt myself let go and relax a bit.

Within a few minutes, and to my genuine surprise, my mind was filled with loving images and thoughts. I was not purposely trying to think such thoughts; they were simply there. I was not attempting to "send love" to anyone, nor trying to make anything happen. Literally, I was simply *seeing something different* — very different — from the appearance of what was going on around me. But it was, somehow, in my experience, much more "real."

The miracle perceives everything as it is.
If nothing but the truth exists,
right-minded seeing cannot see anything but perfection.

—T. p. 34; T-3.II.3:4–5

In my mind I "heard" the little boy say to his mother, "I love you, Mommy," and I "heard" the mother say, "I love you, too, Douglas." I "saw" him settle down and go to sleep peacefully with his head on her lap. Then I "sensed" in some indescribable, non-verbal way, everyone in the car expressing a very simple, basic, underlying love for each other. This vision of love kept expanding until in my heart and mind and experience there was nothing on the entire train — or in the entirety of creation — but love. I felt completely filled with and surrounded by love and was deeply and profoundly moved and grateful.

I then remembered that when the train had first broken down, I had thought of the passage from the Course cited above: that all things work together for good except in the ego's judgment. I had thought that although my ego might judge the breakdown as a negative thing, I could choose to be open to seeing it work for good. I sensed now that the experience of tremendous love I was having was the direct result of having made that choice, although it was not in any way something I "made happen" or could have predicted. It felt rather like a gift of grace and healing.

When I reopened my eyes, I saw that a woman had sat down across the aisle from the mother and was sympathizing with her over how difficult a day and trip this had been for her. The mother was obviously grateful for this understanding and was calming down. A little while later a conductor came by and gently told the mother not to worry, that he was sure there would be no further delays. And a short time after that I looked over and the little boy was asleep with his head in his mother's lap.

These outer events, however, were simply icing on the cake. Had nothing external changed at all, I was certain that healing had been given and received. What I was "shown" when I asked for healing so that I might offer peace was simply a glimpse of the

truth that is always there beneath the layers of fear and forgetfulness that make up this world. For those few minutes, I was certain
of what was real; appearances did not matter and could not affect
that in any way. Later I reflected what a blessing it would be to
live in that awareness all the time.

I was able to choose the healing lesson on the train in a rel-
atively short time, probably because my ego was not greatly
attached to the train being on time. Where our ego attachments
and identifications are greater, so are the fear, distress, and pain
associated in our minds with letting go of how we want things to
be or think they should be.

The Process of Relinquishment —
Looking at Our Attachments

The Course asks us to do nothing more than to look honestly at
the ego and to evaluate fairly what it offers us. For our healing we
do need to let go of the ego, not as an act of sacrifice, but because
we have recognized that what it offers us we do not want. Stripped
of all its elaborate coverings and deceptive defenses, the ego —
which encompasses this entire world of separation — has nothing
to offer us but loss, guilt, scarcity, terror, and death. All its roads
lead there in the end, regardless of how twisting and distracting a
course they seem to take.

Seen clearly, the choice between fear and love, pain and joy, hell
and Heaven, death and life would not be difficult to make. But
we do not see clearly. We have gone deep into the ego's deceptions
and called them home. We are profoundly identified with the ego
and attached to its symbols, especially to the body and sense of
separate self. We fear love, forgiveness, truth, and God, believing
that they demand a sacrifice of us. And we insanely believe that
we can find happiness, safety, security, and peace in a world made
of fear, judgment, attack, illusion, and death.

Yet the idea of "giving up the world" — the things of the world,
the forms of our relationships in the world, our bodies, our ca-

reers, our self-interest and happiness as we define them — fills us with terror. The greater our attachment, the greater our fear of letting go. Defending and clinging to what we have and what we believe we are serves to reinforce our fear. Holding on teaches us we need to be afraid.

However, it is not helpful as students on the spiritual path to pretend that we are not still strongly invested in and attached to our egos, or that we are further along our journey of healing than in fact we are. The Course refers to such pretense as a "particularly unworthy form of denial" (T. p. 20; T-2.IV.3:11). It is unworthy, not in some kind of moral or absolute sense, but because it delays our healing by denying our need for healing.

We will ask for healing and be open to healing — to release from the source of our suffering — only as we accept that we need healing. And so the first step in learning the way of nonattachment, in letting go of the ego, is being willing to look clearly, without judgment or guilt, at how attached we still are to the ego and its many symbols. As we are able, gradually and gently, to release these attachments, we develop deeper and greater trust in a reality beyond the shifting and changing appearances of this world.

All attachment to the ego is, at its core, a defense against — and thus an expression of — fear. To attack ourselves in any way for being afraid only deepens our belief that we have good reason to be afraid. We need to be willing to meet our fear, whatever form it takes, with love. In practice this translates into being accepting, compassionate, and kind to ourselves wherever we are in our process.

This means, as described earlier, being willing to look at our ego from *outside* the ego system — to look at the ego with the Holy Spirit's love rather than with the ego's judgment and condemnation. In this process and experience of stepping back and witnessing our ego attachments, we begin to gradually disidentify from what we are looking at. It is in this way that our attachment to the ego begins to loosen.

Exchanging Nightmares for Happy Dreams

We have already said that, given our strong attachment to the ego, the thought of giving up the world fills us with great fear and seems to entail great sacrifice. And so at this point in our journey, we are not asked to give up the world. Instead we are asked to look at and be truthful about how much pain and fear and conflict we live in much of the time, and gently to be helped to see that there is an alternative we can choose — an alternative that offers us what we *really* want and *truly* value.

> *Our emphasis is not on giving up the world, but on exchanging it for what is far more satisfying, filled with joy, and capable of offering you peace.*
>
> —W. p. 229; W-Pt.I.129.1:3

The Course does teach that this entire world of separation is nothing, a dream, an illusion. In fact, it states that the central thought it attempts to teach is that there is no world (W. p. 237; W-Pt.I.132.6:2–3). Yet at the same time, the Course clearly recognizes that we are not at all ready to accept that teaching fully. This world and our lives here are very real to us in our experience.

We can journey toward truth only by a gentle process that does not increase our fear but lessens it. The goal of the Course is to prepare us to awaken from the dream. The process by which we become ready to awaken is one of allowing our fearful dreams of loss, rejection, abandonment, and punishment to be translated into peaceful dreams of forgiveness and healing that reflect our true and changeless identity as spirit, as perfectly safe and eternally beloved sons and daughters of God.

We are not asked to give up the world. We *are* asked to give up our ego-based judgments and interpretations of the world. The judgments and interpretations we make with our egos inevitably lead us deeper into the darkness of separation, guilt, and fear. We are asked to let these go and let them be replaced with thoughts, perceptions, and interpretations that guide us from darkness to light, despair to hope, conflict to peace, and fear to love. These loving, healing thoughts are *already* in our minds. They are reflections of the One Thought of perfect love God shared with us in and as our creation. We receive them into awareness as we give up the fearful ones we made instead.

Ken Wapnick has pointed out that in this process our lives in this world do not become problem-free in an outward sense. But *we* become happier and more peaceful. We become less anxious, fearful, guilt-ridden, depressed, angry, and plagued by worry and doubt — *regardless* of what happens to be going on in our lives. We develop a sense of *equanimity,* an abiding confidence and calm amid the storms that are part of every human life.

Happy Dreams and the Power of Decision

What the Course means by "happy dreams" is not situations or times in our stories when things turn out the way we think we want them to. Happy dreams are those experiences in which we learn the lesson that nothing can separate us from the peace and love of God but our own choice and that at any moment we can choose again and be restored to love and peace.

Any experience we have in this world can be a classroom in which we learn that lesson, if that is what we are willing to learn. *Every* experience offers us the chance to reclaim the power we have projected onto outer circumstances to determine our peace of mind and heart. At the same time, the Course recognizes and reminds us that "it takes great learning to understand that all events, encounters and circumstances are helpful" (M. p. 9; M-4.I.4:5).

It is important for us to recognize that we have not already achieved that level of mastery and understanding. We all still react to a great many events, encounters, and circumstances with our ego, judging them as negative, as loss. We are quick to perceive threat and attack and to respond with anger, defensiveness, and fear. We interpret events, situations, and circumstances as "proof" of the "reality" of sin, guilt, and punishment. We believe that our safety, security, and peace depend on our controlling and dictating the outer circumstances of our lives.

We open the way to greater healing as we begin to recognize how painful the ego's perceptions of the world are to us, as well as recognize how strongly attracted we are to those perceptions and interpretations. Our minds gravitate again and again to that way of seeing and thinking.

Yet we are not helpless, powerless victims of our own thoughts. Our thoughts do not happen to us, although it may, and often does, seem that way. We think those thoughts and we continue thinking them. We can also decide that we want to think differently. This requires developing a level of mental discipline that most of us have not yet fully achieved. Yet we can achieve it, through willingness and practice.

The Course does not require us to accept these teachings at face value as true. It does ask that we apply the teachings and let our own experience teach us if they are true. It is the peace and release from fear and pain we experience when we ask for and accept the Holy Spirit's way of seeing in place of the ego's that becomes our incentive to continue on this journey of healing.

Our confidence, trust, and faith gradually deepen as we turn to Him more and more often, asking to share His thoughts, His perspective, His understanding, His peace. Little by little we learn that this peace is all that we truly value, all that we truly want. Ego attachments rob us of peace. As we become clearer about what we really want, we become more willing to look at our ego attachments honestly and let them go.

Practicing Equanimity — a Personal Experience

Shortly after I first began writing about learning nonattachment and equanimity, in February 1992, a situation occurred in my own life that gave me a chance — or forced me — to directly apply the ideas I was writing about. At that time I found myself suddenly, and unexpectedly, confronted with a conflict involving my apartment in New York City. I perceived the situation as a threat, not only to my home of sixteen years, but to my work life, income, and routine as well. I reacted with immediate fear and anticipation of loss, projecting my worst fears into the future. Although I knew on some level that my reaction was out of proportion both to the information I had and to the situation itself, emotionally I plunged into a sense of doom and despair.

Even as this was occurring, I fleetingly thought it interesting and ironic that I was in the midst of writing about learning nonattachment. I had the faintest glimmer of recognition that this situation might be a lesson and opportunity for healing, regardless of the outcome. But for the most part I was not living within that possibility and perspective. I was certainly not experiencing any sense of equanimity or peace. I was miserable and frightened. I was clearly attached to how I wanted things to be, how I wanted the situation to be resolved, and I was definitely judging with my ego. As far as I was concerned, this was a terrible situation. I was caught up in perceiving my happiness, peace, and well-being as dependent on my external circumstances.

And yet that faint glimmer of awareness that this experience might be used for good, for learning, for healing — though nearly drowned out by my ego's proclamations of disaster and forecasts of doom — was enough to set the healing and learning process in motion.

Recognizing the Real Problem

A problem cannot be solved if you do not know what it is. Even if it is already solved you will still have the problem, because you will not recognize that it has been solved. This is the situation of the world. The problem of separation, which is really the only problem, has already been solved. Yet the solution is not recognized because the problem is not recognized.

—W. p. 139; W-Pt.I.79.1

I try to begin each morning with quiet time for reading, reflection, prayer, and/or meditation. The morning after I had learned about the problem with my apartment, I woke up very fearful and upset. It was very apparent that I needed to get quiet and ask for help to see differently.

What became clear to me was what the problem really was. The problem was *not* the situation with my apartment. The problem, the real cause of my upset and fear, was that I felt *alone* in facing the situation. I was not feeling God's presence and love supporting, guiding, and sustaining me. I was relying on my own perception, understanding, and experience to deal with what *I* had defined as the problem — and I was obviously doubtful of my ability to deal with it effectively.

The Course points out that if we are trusting in our own strength to deal with the problems of life, we have every reason to be apprehensive and fearful. Our ego-based perceptions and judgments are inherently limited and distorted and will lead us further into the experience of conflict and separation.

Whenever a situation is causing us concern or anxiety, we can be sure that we are trying to understand and solve it with our ego. We cannot help, on some level, but feel inadequate. There is, however, a deeper wisdom and strength within us that we can turn to and draw upon instead.

> *It is obvious that any situation that causes you concern is associated with feelings of inadequacy, for otherwise you would believe that you could deal with the situation successfully. It is not by trusting yourself that you will gain confidence. But the strength of God in you is successful in all things.*
>
> —W. p. 75; W-Pt.I.47.5:2–4

As I recognized the real source of my fear, my sense of separation from God's strength and love within me, I also saw clearly that the answer was to turn back to that Presence. My prayer became asking for help in choosing to join with God's Love within me, as my fear was ample evidence that I had already chosen to join with the ego instead. Almost immediately I experienced a calming down inside, a feeling of reassurance and peace.

From that perspective, I saw the situation with my apartment as simply a situation that needed to be dealt with and resolved, not as something I had to be frightened of or threatened by. I felt very grateful for that perception and release from fear and for a deeper understanding and acceptance of the Course's teaching that there is "one problem, one solution" (W. p. 141; W-Pt.I.80.1:5).

Letting Go of Attachment to the Outcome

However, as the Course points out, "readiness...is not mastery" (M. p. 14; M-4.IX.1:10). Despite the peace and relief I experienced when I chose to join with God's loving presence in my mind, the Holy Spirit, rather than with the ego's voice of fear, I did not consistently maintain that choice. Over the next several days, I went back into anxiety and fear a great deal of the time. In retrospect, it seems that there was more inner work for me to do, more healing and learning potential in the situation than I had tapped that first morning.

Although I had recognized the need to be open to feeling God's presence with and within me, I also still had a strong attachment to how I wanted the situation with my apartment to be resolved. I realized how much I liked the way things had been — how comfortable, convenient, pleasant, workable, and secure it felt to me. I did not want to give that up, to "lose" all of that.

I was looking at those people who appeared to be threatening my comfortable status quo as enemies whom I needed to watch out for and to outmaneuver. Every decision I made and action I took from that fear-based state of mind only seemed to me to backfire, complicate things, make the situation even worse. I found myself becoming increasingly fearful as the days went by and no resolution appeared to be forthcoming.

During this time I worked with a series of Workbook lessons

from the Course (Lessons 128 through 133) that were tremendously helpful in directing my attention back to my own mind and perception, rather than the outer situation, as the source of what I was feeling and going through. They reminded me that I needed, first and foremost, to change my mind about the situation I was in, to let it be an opportunity for healing and release, another chance to learn that my peace, happiness, security, and well-being lie within, not in the outer circumstances of my life.

We said earlier that what the Course means by "happy dreams" is *not* those times when the circumstances of our lives are to our liking. In fact, the Course points out, such situations keep us bound to the world of separation and fear just as much as those in which our circumstances seem to cause us pain. Both reinforce the seeming reality of separation and with it the ego's entire thought system of guilt, pain, suffering, fear, loss, and death.

> *The dreams you think you like would hold you back as much as those in which the fear is seen. For every dream is but a dream of fear, no matter what the form it seems to take. The fear is seen within, without, or both. Or it can be disguised in pleasant form. But never is it absent from the dream, for fear is the material of dreams, from which they are all made. Their form can change, but they cannot be made of something else.*
>
> —T. p. 569; T-29.IV.2:1–6

This experience in my life — in which circumstances I very much liked were being threatened — helped me to see that investing my sense of happiness and well-being into these circumstances had subtly fed an underlying foundation of insecurity and fear. In this world everything eventually changes, because this is a world of change. As long as we seek lasting peace and safety in anything of the world, we will one day be disappointed and experience loss, even if we seem temporarily to succeed in having what we want.

The Course teaches that we can find the abiding happiness, safety, and love we seek only in what is changeless: in the reality of our true Self, in our identity as God created us, in the peace of God that is our inheritance.

I began to see that as long as I was attached to a particular outcome in form, I would remain trapped in fear. If what I wanted was in conflict with what the other people involved wanted, I would inevitably see them as the enemy trying to hurt or deprive me. I would continue to experience threat and fear, plot my strategy and defense, anticipate their retaliation and counterattack. There was no doubt in my mind or my heart that this was living in hell.

It became very clear that I did not want to continue seeing the other people involved in this situation as enemies. Once I had made this inner decision, I found my perception of them starting to shift. Where I had perceived conflict, I began to see misunderstanding. Where I had perceived a need for strategy and defense, I began to see the need for correction and communication. My experience of the situation began to shift dramatically, and I found it easier and less stressful to take the appropriate action I needed to take to move toward resolution.

I also began to let go of my attachment to the outcome of the situation. I certainly still had a preference of how I thought I wanted it to turn out, but I also recognized that that was my ego's evaluation and conclusion. I realized that I honestly did not know what was best for everyone in the situation, but *whatever* it was, I knew that on a deeper level I wanted that.

I wanted healing, I wanted love, I wanted release from the pain of separation and fear. I did not know how to get there. But I knew there was a Wisdom within me that did, and I wanted that Answer in place of my own. As I let go into trust, I again experienced a deeper sense of peace.

Looking at the Guilt in Our Minds

One morning during this time, I awoke very early in a state of actual panic. In desperation I began to write down my thoughts, as that is often a useful tool for me to look at and accept my ego thoughts rather than dig myself deeper into a hole of self-judgment and recrimination.

Initially I was horrified at what I was writing. The intensity of self-accusation, guilt, and self-hatred pouring out onto the paper was overwhelming. As I continued to write — and asked the Holy Spirit to look at these thoughts with me — I began to be able to step back away from them. As I withdrew identification from them, they began to lose intensity and energy. The only power they had was the belief and reality I invested in them.

I had realized from the start that my emotional reaction to the situation with my apartment was objectively out of proportion to the event, even at the level of the world. What I became aware of as I wrote was that I had, in my mind, turned this situation into a *symbol* of enormous unconscious guilt and the resulting terror of punishment.

I knew that morning that this guilt was not about anything that had ever occurred in the story line of this life. It was not about anything that had happened in my childhood or my personal history. It was as if I were looking straight into a cauldron of raw, existential unworthiness, guilt, and terror that were built into the very nature and fabric of my mind.

The Course teaches that the healing process is one of looking at the insane guilt that is the bedrock of the ego's thought system with the love of the Holy Spirit next to us to uphold us and teach us it is not real. As painful as that morning was, it was also very healing. I saw, unmasked for a time, what the ego is really offering me — and I also saw that I have a choice. There is another Voice within my mind that I can listen to instead, a Voice that offers me profound acceptance, healing, and peace.

Sorting Out the Valuable from the Valueless

I had a chance to practice that choice the following day, when I worked with Lesson 133: "I will not value what is valueless"

(W. pp. 239–41; W-Pt.I.133). I became aware that what was really valueless were the thoughts of my ego — the thoughts of anxiety, the pictures of fear I was projecting into the future, etc. They offered me nothing that I really want. What I wanted, and the only thing of any real value, was the peace of God. Throughout the day, each time my mind would go in the direction of fear — which was often — I would remind myself that I would not value what was valueless, that I would not value those thoughts by continuing to dwell on them, and that I wanted the peace of God instead. Each time, I was answered with peace.

The outer situation with my apartment was resolved through the problem simply fading away over the next several weeks. But the clarification of my real goal, peace, was the greatest learning and gift for me through the whole experience. I came to realize that what I really wanted was inner peace, regardless of what was going on around me, and that peace was truly possible, even while a challenging situation in my life remained unresolved. I am very grateful for the gift of that living discovery and practical awareness.

I have no sense that I have gone beyond the very beginning stages of learning and mastering the qualities of nonattachment and equanimity. Life since then has continued to afford me opportunities and challenges, both small and great, to practice and deepen this learning. What I do have now is a deeper faith and deeper sense than before that such mastery is possible for us, that we can experience the peace of God more and more in our lives, and that in doing so we can fulfill our function here, that of helping each other remember home.

Chapter 9

Straw into Gold:
The Way of Choosing Blessing

> *Although the world is full of suffering,*
> *it is also full of the overcoming of it.*
>
> — HELEN KELLER

> *In each and every aspect of life, the chance to turn the straw*
> *we find there into gold is there in our hearts.... When we*
> *see with eyes of wisdom, difficulties can become our good*
> *fortune.*
>
> — JACK KORNFIELD, *A Path with Heart*

Coming to terms with the difficulties and painful experiences that happen in life is an essential part of the spiritual journey, and especially of cultivating equanimity. In the fall of 1994 I saw a fascinating television interview with Gloria Vanderbilt. After describing tragedy after tragedy that had occurred over the course of Vanderbilt's life, the interviewer asked her if she ever found herself thinking, "Why me?" Vanderbilt's answer was striking. "Well, why not me?" she replied matter-of-factly. "Suffering and tragedy are a part of every human life. What would make me think that I should somehow be immune?"

I was struck by the maturity of insight and understanding in this statement. Adversity *is* a part of this human experience, a part of every human life. We have noted before that compassion is born of this very awareness and recognition.

Pain seems a very personal and private universe while we are going through it. It can seem to make us different, separate, and isolated from those around us. Yet all that we suffer is part of the greater suffering of humankind, of all that lives in this separated existence.

> *Such strength of heart comes from knowing that the pain we each must bear is a part of the greater pain shared by all that lives. It is not just "our" pain but the pain, and realizing this awakens our universal compassion. In this way our suffering opens our hearts.*
>
> — JACK KORNFIELD, *A Path with Heart*

The compassion that is awakened in us needs also to extend to *ourselves,* to how we view and understand the difficulties and challenges in our own lives. Psychologist John Welwood, a Buddhist practitioner, has speculated that the prevalence of depression in our Western world stems in part from our lack of acceptance and appreciation of adversity as a natural part of life.

Rather than recognize that problems are part and parcel of life in this world, we tend to judge that having problems is *itself* a problem. We often view our problems and difficulties as a source of embarrassment or shame, a failure, an indictment of us, evidence or proof of our basic lack of worth. Spiritual and metaphysical teachings are often used — or, more accurately, misused — to reinforce this idea and compound the pain we are already experiencing.

Yet, the fact is that we have all faced times of hardship, difficulty, suffering, and loss, and we will most likely face such times again in the course of our lives. For those on the spiritual path, periods of darkness, doubt, and discouragement — even despair — are part of the faith journey at some time or other. How we face these kinds of experiences in our lives and in the development of our faith or spiritual practice, how we define them and what we tell ourselves they mean, will largely determine what they turn out to be for us. They can either be a curse that plagues, diminishes, and defeats us, or a blessing from which we emerge spiritually stronger, wiser, more mature, more compassionate, more whole.

Jack Kornfield writes, "It is the power of the heart to encounter any difficult circumstance and turn it into a golden opportunity" (*A Path with Heart*). The Course teaches that there is a way of looking at *everything* that happens in this world and in our lives that lets it be for us a step closer to God (W. p. 359; W-Pt.I.193.13:1).

Often it is the painful times in our lives that force us to undertake, or deepen, our spiritual search. When things are going well, we may believe that we're in control of our lives and that we don't need anything beyond ourselves. It is also easy to profess faith in God when the circumstances of our lives are basically to our liking. Adversity often shakes our faith — whether this is faith in ourselves or in God — and forces us to seek a deeper truth for our lives, a deeper and more solid foundation for our inner peace.

> *Pain is often the stimulus that brings spiritual growth and transformation. Sorrow can enhance our compassion and open us to a larger reality. A broken heart can become an open heart.... When suffering enters your life, you can use it to grow spiritually — or remain victimized by it. In this choice your real freedom lies.*
>
> — DOUGLAS BLOCH, *I Am with You Always*

Hard as it may be at times for us to accept or believe, there are *no exceptions* to this fundamental spiritual principle: that *everything* that happens in this life can bring us closer to God and to the joy of realizing our own true nature. Everything can be used for growth, for healing, for good. But it is *up to us* whether we will let the storms, the crises, even the tragedies we suffer in our lives be used for this purpose.

Near the end of their wandering in the desert, Moses crystallized the heart of his teachings to the Israelites in this way: "I have set before you this day death and life, blessing and curse. There-fore choose life, choose blessing, that you and those who come after you may fully live" (Deut. 30:19). This power to choose blessing instead of curse — to affirm life and love even in the face of the harsh appearances of destruction and death — is, the Course teaches, the *one real power* we have as human beings. It is a power that no one and nothing outside can take away from us. But it is also a power that only we ourselves can exercise. No one can make our choice for us.

The Meaning Something Has for Us Is a Choice We Make

We take a strong stand for our own empowerment when we rec-ognize that we give meaning, definition, and purpose to the things that happen in our lives — and that it is the meaning we give that ultimately determines how we will experience these events and sit-uations. The meaning something has for us is, in reality, a choice that we ourselves make.

This is illustrated in a light-hearted way by the following story.

A little boy was overheard talking to himself as he strode through his backyard, baseball cap in place and toting ball and bat. "I'm the greatest baseball player in the world," he said proudly. Then he tossed the ball up in the air, swung and missed. Undaunted, he picked up the ball, threw it into the air and said to himself, "I'm the greatest player ever!" He swung at the ball again, and again he missed. He paused a moment to examine bat and ball carefully. Then once again he threw the ball into the air and said, "I'm the greatest base-ball player who ever lived." He swung the bat hard and again missed the ball.

"Wow!" he exclaimed. "What a pitcher!"

— SOURCE UNKNOWN, QUOTED IN *Chicken Soup for the Soul,* WRITTEN AND COMPILED BY J. CANFIELD AND M. HANSEN

We are meaning-seeking creatures. We seek orientation, trying to make sense out of the things that happen to us and other
people. As we go through our lives, we are continually asking and
answering the question "What is happening here? Why is it happening? What does it mean?" What does this mean, we are really
asking, about who we are, about life, about God?

Spiritual Deepening

*I think what has deepened my experience of God had to do
with my parents' message to me that every event was something that God was participating in.... The Biblical line in
Job is "Afflictions heal and adversity opens you to a new reality." So how do I deepen my experience of God? Through
afflictions and adversity.... I think it's hard to deepen your
experience when nothing goes wrong.*

— BERNIE SIEGEL, QUOTED IN *Bridges to Heaven,*
ED. JONATHAN ROBINSON

Albert Einstein once remarked that the most important question
a human being must ask and answer is, "Is the universe a friendly
place?" Is life basically benevolent? Is God truly loving? Am I being guided and watched over, supported and loved? Whether we
are conscious of the process or not, in every moment and every
situation we are asking and answering for ourselves these basic,
fundamental questions.

Hardship, difficulty, and tragedy have a way of heightening
these questions, of forcing us to look at our most basic as-
sumptions, beliefs, and fears about life, God, and our own true
nature. Joan Borysenko, in her book *Fire in the Soul,* states that
tragedy brings forth in us a need to create meaning, to answer the
questions "Why me?" or "Why this?"

Borysenko points out that our answers to these questions will
be either basically pessimistic or basically optimistic. If what we
tell ourselves about painful and challenging experiences in our

lives reinforces a pessimistic outlook and self-perception, our ability to effectively deal with, recover from, and make use of these experiences is seriously compromised. We can get stuck in anger, fear, or bitterness that can make it difficult, if not impossible, to go on with really living our lives in a full, satisfying, and happy way.

If, on the other hand, the explanations and answers we give ourselves are more affirming — if we can genuinely accept that there is a potential for growth and blessing in the situation, even if we cannot yet see what it is or imagine how we could ever actualize it — then our human suffering is likely to contain the seeds of spiritual awakening, transformation, and healing.

The story in the Gospel of John of the man born blind illustrates these two very different perceptions of the same situation. In this story, Jesus' disciples assumed that the man's blindness was a punishment for sin. They wanted Jesus to tell them *whose* sins were being punished: the man's own sins or those of his parents. Jesus answered that the man's blindness was not a punishment at all but rather an opportunity for the power of God to be manifested.

When we are willing to view a situation of hardship or suffering in our lives as an opportunity to become more aware of the presence and power of God, of love, in our lives — even when we cannot imagine how that could possibly come about — we open the doorway for growth and healing. We are likely to be able someday to look back on the experience as an *initiation* into a deepened or enhanced capacity to love and be loved. And we will discover that we have emerged from this initiation, not diminished by it as we may have feared we would be, but *more* than we were before. We'll find that we have become more compassionate, more connected to our real values, more in touch with our inner strength, more alive.

Whether it pleases us or not, each moment is a gift. No matter how unpleasant the wrapping, inside is something wonderful that life wants to give us. If we let it pass without opening it, we have missed something priceless.

— POLLY BERRIEN BERENDS, *Coming to Life*

Rarely do we start out seeing the gift or welcoming the opportunity offered us by the painful challenges and difficulties in life. Our first, human response to such situations is more likely to be resistance of some sort: anger, fear, depression, blame. Our initial definition and feeling is likely to be at least somewhat pessimistic. We may feel, on some level, that we are being punished, either justly or unjustly. We may feel singled out, victimized, helpless, abandoned, or betrayed.

We may feel like we're trapped in a nightmare, as though we've been plunged into a place of darkness and fear from which there seems to be no means of escape. How do we make our way out of that terribly painful psychological and spiritual place when we find ourselves there?

Choosing and coming to blessing in these kinds of experiences is a *process*. We arrive at awareness of blessing; we do not start there. We travel a journey of healing, which both calls forth and asks of us a deep courage, faith, patience, and sincerity of effort.

The Process of Choosing Blessing

The process of healing from painful experiences in our lives — the process of choosing blessing — will be manifest differently in every situation. Yet as I reflect on experiences in my own life, there do seem to be some general principles or guidelines that have been helpful in facilitating and cooperating with this process.

These are not consecutive steps, to be done once, in a particular order. Nor are they a "formula for healing." They are simply ways of thinking, reminders, that I have found helpful to draw upon and practice in times of challenge and healing.

1. Be honest about how you feel and what you are really telling yourself.

It is extremely important not to deny or whitewash what's really going on inside of us in an effort to "be spiritual" or appear "enlightened." Doing so merely keeps those thoughts and feelings away from the light of healing and prolongs our suffering.

It is very difficult to reach a desired destination if you deceive yourself about where you are starting from. I recently began reading a wonderful book by Buddhist teacher Pema Chodron, entitled *Start Where You Are*. There really is nowhere else you *can* start. You may not like your starting point, but you do need to tell the truth about what it is.

Feeling and accepting the feelings we have does not mean justifying them, glorifying them, or having to act on them. It does mean accepting ourselves feeling those feelings, thinking those thoughts, forgiving ourselves, and having compassion for the pained and fearful state of mind we are in.

2. Recognize that there is a price you pay for continuing to hold on to those feelings, thoughts, and definitions of the situation.

While anger, blaming, feelings of victimization, even a desire for revenge, may be natural first reactions to painful experiences in our lives, we need to recognize that we pay a price for continuing to hold on to these kinds of feelings. In *Fire in the Soul,* Joan Borysenko points out that research indicates that people who see themselves as helpless victims and people who harbor blaming or self-blaming attitudes are more susceptible to decreased immune function, increased heart disease, and a host of stress-related disorders.

There is an old saying that acid corrodes the vessel in which it is stored. While anger sometimes seems to give us a feeling of power and strength, this feeling is illusory. In reality anger disempowers and weakens us. Dr. Borysenko describes a kinesiology, or muscle testing, demonstration that she has used that graphically illustrates this point.

In this demonstration, a volunteer is asked to stand with his stronger arm extending straight out from his shoulder. He is told to resist the experimenter's effort to push the arm down. This establishes a baseline of normal muscle strength. The volunteer is then asked to repeat the procedure, but this time to gather his strength by closing his eyes and concentrating on something that really makes him angry. He signals that he has the image clearly in focus by nodding his head. The experimenter once again presses down on the volunteer's arm, which inevitably collapses with very little effort. Finally the volunteer is asked to repeat the process a third time. This time he is asked to focus his mind on something or someone he really loves. Now it is nearly impossible to move the arm at all, even with great exertion on the part of the experimenter. The volunteer's own experience is that his ability to maintain his arm position this third time through is generally quite effortless.

I was already familiar with the general process of muscle testing and decided to try this experiment for myself. So far, I have tested it with over twenty volunteers, all men and all taller, heavier, and stronger than I am. The results have been dramatic and strikingly consistent. Anger weakens us, drains our vital energy, and saps our life force. Having love as our focus strengthens and empowers us in a profound way. When we begin to recognize and really feel the truth of this, we reach a point of *wanting* to let go of our angry feelings and perceptions and wanting sincerely to redirect the energy of our thoughts to love.

3. Set the goal of healing.

The year 1994 began for me with a time of great personal upheaval and transition. My emotions were raw and ran the gamut of what I described earlier. Yet from the beginning, even in the midst of anger, fear, and pain, my prayer was "Let this experience be for healing."

I was very clear that I did not simply want to "grit my teeth" and manage to "get through" the changes that had become necessary in my life. I had done that before in similar situations, and nothing had really changed inside me. I found myself experiencing the same fears, repeating the same patterns of defense, living out the same beliefs, again and again.

This time I knew I wanted something more. I wanted to *heal* through this experience, to come out the other side with a much greater sense of freedom, openness to love, and happiness than I had known before in my life. I prayed that prayer for healing many, many times over the months that followed.

The clarity of the goal in my mind and heart became a star for me, a point of light that helped to steady, guide, and reassure me at the times when my inner experience grew darkest. On some level I trusted and knew that the outcome of this transition in my life would be healing — even when I could not imagine what that might look like or how I would ever get there.

The Course teaches that the best time to set a goal is at the beginning. But we also need to remember that, in a sense, we are *always* at the beginning. This moment — every moment — is fresh and new. Every moment offers us an opportunity to change our perception. Every moment offers us the chance to set the goal of healing.

To set the goal of healing is to align ourselves with God's Will and purpose for this situation in our lives. God's Will cannot fail to be manifest in our experience once we have accepted that it is our own as well. Once we have set the goal of healing, the outcome must be healing. The timing and the route may be unknown, but the outcome is certain.

4. Affirm God's presence and God's power to bring forth healing from this experience.

It is easy to have "faith" when things are going well. It is easy to see God's reflection in what is loving, beautiful, and harmonious. To affirm God's presence and love where it is not obvious or apparent draws us to a deeper level of faith and opens us to a more profound spiritual receptivity and vision.

Reminding ourselves that there is a wisdom and power beyond that of our ego operating in our lives can be particularly helpful and comforting during times of difficulty. Many years ago, I found myself facing a situation that brought up intense feelings of anxiety, shame, and hopelessness in me. The situation involved substantial debts that had been accrued by my former husband while we were married. While legally I was jointly liable for these debts, they were far beyond what my level of personal income would enable me to repay. I could see no possible solution or resolution, no way out of the mess I was in. I had to meet with one of the creditors, and I was filled with fear.

At the time I was just beginning to work with metaphysical principles and to explore the ways that my consciousness impacted my outer experience. As part of this exploration, I read some of Catherine Ponder's writings on prosperity. She suggested one affirmation that almost jumped right off the page at me. It spoke directly to my real need, seemed to open up a whole new universe of possibility for me, and brought me a great sense of comfort and peace. That affirmation, based on a passage from the Psalms, said

> *Be still and know that I am God,*
> *at work in this situation.*

It had not occurred to me that God's hand — a deeper love and wisdom — could be at work in this problem situation. It certainly didn't look that way to me. Yet something within me opened to that possibility and I felt deeply reassured. I felt hopeful that a solution existed, even if I could not see it from where I stood. Over the next few years that situation did resolve itself, and I have continued to find this affirmation of God's presence and power to be a helpful reminder time and time again.

Another helpful reminder for me has been the story of Joseph and his brothers in the Book of Genesis. Joseph's brothers had grown extremely jealous of their father's love for their youngest brother. One day they attacked him, stole his beautiful coat, and left him for dead in a ditch. Passersby found him and sold him into slavery.

He ended up in the court of Egypt, where his ability to interpret the pharaoh's troubling dreams won him his freedom and a place of honor as a trusted advisor to the pharaoh. Many years later his brothers came to the court, seeking food to take back to their country, which had been ravaged by famine. They did not recognize Joseph, but he knew them.

Joseph was moved by pity for their plight and by the love he still felt for them and for his father. He gave them what they asked and then revealed his identity to them. They were astounded by his kindness, generosity, and forgiveness after the evil they had done to him. He answered them, simply, "You may have intended it for evil, but God intended it for good."

However we came to be in whatever situation of adversity we are in, even if it was through a destructive, hurtful intent on the part of someone else or ourselves, we need to be open to the possibility and remind ourselves that God intends it — that is, God can use it — for healing, for blessing, for good.

5. Ask for help.

The Course is very clear that from the perspective of our ego we cannot see the blessing that problems and situations of adversity or suffering hold for us. We need to ask for help, to reach out to a source of wisdom that is outside of our egocentric perception and perspective. We need to ask the Holy Spirit, our inner teacher, to correct the misperceptions we are holding that are causing us suffering, to help us see the blessing and healing in the situation. The Holy Spirit can "answer" us in the quiet of our meditation or prayer time; through the guidance and support of loving friends or counselors; through things we read that seem to have been written just for our need; through music we listen to, conversations we overhear, or countless other seemingly serendipitous ways.

God answers us sometimes with insight and understanding, other times with the gifts of courage and inner strength. We may be answered with a stirring of inspiration or hope, ideas of new directions and possibilities, or a feeling of being comforted and reassured that we are loved. The Course teaches that God's answer is always some form of peace.

One of my favorite passages from the Course states, "If you knew Who walks beside you on the way that you have chosen, fear would be impossible" (T. p. 353; T-18.III.3:2). Part of the suffering we go through in the trials of life is feeling that we are alone in what we are facing. Yet we are told that "mighty companions" journey with us on our path, healing, upholding, supporting, and reinforcing every step we take. Reaching out and asking for help opens us to the possibility of learning that, in fact, we are not alone.

God has promised that we will never be left comfortless. But we need to reach out and ask.

6. Be open to the healing process as it reveals itself.

The Course asks us not to dictate to God the way He should come to us, reminding us gently that He knows the way. We set the goal of healing, but the means are given — revealed — to us.

The process of healing from a painful experience may not look the way we think it will, or should. It may include seeming setbacks, delays, and unexpected and surprising turns in the road.

I recently read a very moving story about a couple whose teenage son had been killed by a drunk driver. The driver was convicted and sentenced to a lengthy prison term. The driver's own son, a young boy, was terminally ill and had only a short time left to live. The man pleaded with the judge to delay the start of his sentence so he could spend the last few months of his child's life with him.

The parents of the boy who had been killed had been, until this time, consumed with grief, rage, and outrage toward the driver. They argued strongly and passionately against the judge granting leniency in the start of his prison time. Then, suddenly, one morning the mother knew in her heart that she needed to ask the judge to grant the request. She "knew" inside that for her own healing

she needed to offer this man what she had not had — the chance
to spend the last moments of a son's life with him.

She shared this feeling with her husband who, miraculously,
had come to the same recognition within himself. They went before the judge and supported the request that the man's sentence
be delayed until after his little boy's death. Everyone involved was
deeply affected by this expression of compassion, understanding,
and forgiveness. For the parents, too, it was a profound experience
of healing.

It is important that we not judge the process of our healing:
how long it takes, what it looks like, what it might include. It is
also helpful not to prejudge certain processes (like prayer, meditation, and other spiritual approaches) as being acceptable and
others (like support groups, therapy, medication, or concrete life
changes) as being unacceptable. We need to do the best we can to
be inwardly honest, open, and receptive to direction from God's
Voice, from our own deep wisdom, and to let the healing process
unfold and reveal itself to us step by step.

7. Don't give up until you've received the blessing.

There is a humorous story told of a little girl who was incurably
optimistic. One day she was put into a room filled nearly to the
ceiling with horse manure. A few hours later she was discovered
to be digging quite happily and contentedly through the manure.
When asked what on earth she was doing, she cheerfully replied,
"Well, with all this manure, I figure there's got to be a pony in
here somewhere!"

Over the last few years I've been very taken by the story of Jacob wrestling with the angel of God. They struggled all night, and
Jacob was wounded in the process. As dawn approached, the angel tried to pull away, for he had to return to Heaven by daylight.
Jacob held tightly to him and insisted, "I won't release you until
you give me a blessing." The angel blessed Jacob and gave him a
new name. He became Israel — "one who has struggled with the
angel of God and prevailed."

We need to be like Jacob: to not give up, to keep inwardly grappling, in a sense, with the unhealed, unresolved situations in our lives and our psyches, until we have received the blessing they hold for us. Only when we have received the blessing have we truly come to a deeper knowing of who we really are. Only then do we go forward in our lives with a "new name" — a fuller and greater realization and expression of our own spiritual truth.

When our healing from a painful experience is complete, we find that we actually feel grateful for the experience as a part of our lives. That does not mean we would ask or want to go through it again. It simply means that we are at peace with what occurred, because we have fully received the blessings it contained for us.

When we are in the midst of a painful situation and while it remains unresolved or unhealed, it may be nearly impossible to conceive of ever experiencing gratitude or blessing from the situation. The following prayer, found scribbled on a piece of wrapping paper near the body of a dead child at the Ravensbruck concentration camp, speaks to the profound expansive potential of our spirit for healing.

> *O Lord,*
> *remember not only*
> *the men and women of good will,*
> *but also those of evil will.*
> *But remember not all the suffering*
> *they have inflicted upon us;*
> *remember the fruits we have borne*
> *thanks to this suffering—*
> *our comradeship,*
> *our loyalty,*
> *our humility,*
> *our courage,*
> *our generosity,*
> *the greatness of heart*
> *which has grown out of all this;*
> *and when they come to the judgement,*

let all the fruits that we have borne
be their forgiveness.

— FROM *Praying Their Faith: An Insight*
into Six World Religions through
the Prayers of Their Members

If we do not yet feel grateful and fully at peace with a situation in our lives, it simply means there is more healing to be accomplished in us. We have not yet received the blessing. We need both to be patient with ourselves and persistent in our desire and intention for healing. Let's not give up on ourselves short of the blessing. There is a pony in there somewhere.

8. Remember that your healing is not for you alone.

There is a beautiful spiritual teacher named Patricia Sun, whom I have heard speak many times over the years. I remember clearly Patricia once saying to us in a workshop:

> *I deeply wish that whenever you find yourself right up against your edges of fear — those places of darkness that are most painful to you and most frightening — I wish so much that at those times you could feel my gratitude and love for you. For those places are what you have agreed to take on for healing, not only in your own consciousness, but for the whole of human consciousness. And I wish you could feel at those moments how grateful I am to you for your willingness and courage to take on that piece of our healing.*

Buddhist tradition teaches that dedicating our own experiences of suffering to the healing of others, of all living beings who suffer, can bring a sense of meaning and purpose to the painful challenges inherent in our human lives.

The Course also teaches that when we are healed, we are not healed alone. When we choose blessing instead of curse, when we choose healing to come from the experience of brokenness, we choose it not only for ourselves but for our brothers and sisters as well. At the deepest level, all minds and hearts are joined.

As we demonstrate that pain can give way to joy, anger to forgiveness, and anguish to love, our lives become examples of that possibility for everyone. And we receive the gratitude and thanks of all creation. For we have remembered a bit more clearly who we really are — and that is the one blessing that contains them all.

The Gentle Smile

Without your smile,
the world cannot be saved.

—W. p. 177; W-Pt.I.100.3:3

The source of a true smile
is an awakened mind.

— THICH NHAT HANH

As we develop and deepen in our practice of loving kindness, compassion, sympathetic joy, nonattachment and equanimity, our lives begin to take on a truly remarkable quality of being. This quality can be described as "the gentle smile."

The Course describes,

There is a way of living in the world that is not here, although it seems to be. You do not change appearance, though you smile more frequently.

—W. p. 284; W-Pt.I.155.1:1–2

And Thich Nhat Hanh writes,

155

A tiny bud of a smile on our lips nourishes awareness and calms us miraculously. It returns us to the peace we thought we had lost.

— THICH NHAT HANH, *Peace Is Every Step*

The gentle smile is the smile of a peaceful heart. It is a smile of awareness, humor, freedom, and boundless love. The gentle smile reflects a state of mind that sees beyond the illusory appearances of separation, that sees deeply into the true nature of things.

The gentle smile is a smile of recognition of our interconnectedness with each other and with all that lives. It is a smile of gratitude for our complete dependence upon and union with the Reality and Source of our existence and being.

Literally, when we smile the muscles in our face relax. Even on a physical level, a gentle smile is a letting go, an undoing of tension and effort. As we choose to smile, we relax into the joy of our deeper nature. As we practice the gentle smile, on all levels we teach ourselves peace.

Practice

Life and people afford us a wealth of opportunities each day to practice the gentle smile. Countless times a day, in our interactions and in our thoughts, we choose between intensifying separation and conflict or being a vehicle for peace. As we become more mindful, we realize just how often we need to decide between making a "big deal" out of something silly or, instead, letting it go.

Certainly there are times when issues and problems between people need to be addressed directly. But as we learn to do this from the love in our hearts, from a place of compassion and kindness that recognizes and respects all that we have in common despite our conflicts, we find that we move more gracefully and gently toward the harmonious resolution of difficulties.

Humanly we will find some situations, relationships, and conflicts more difficult and challenging than others. If we are willing to practice the gentle smile in situations that are not as highly charged emotionally, we gradually develop our ability to return to peace in situations that we find more challenging as well.

Freedom

Our ability to smile is an expression of our real freedom. In the ego-mind, we think we need a reason to smile. We think that our smile depends on the outer conditions of our lives. If things are good, we can smile. If things are not good, how can we possibly smile? Choosing the gentle smile teaches us that we are greater than the circumstances of our lives.

Nothing outside can bring us happiness or peace. Nothing outside can rob us of happiness or peace. In any moment, whatever is happening, we can choose healing instead of separation, love instead of fear, peace instead of turmoil and strife. In any moment we can choose to smile. Nothing can steal our smile. It is always within us. This is the truth that makes us free.

Awareness

The gentle smile is a smile of awareness. In this moment, I am here, I am *alive*. I do not have to go anywhere or seek anything. I can breathe and experience life and the present moment, and I can smile.

Thich Nhat Hanh suggests that we take a few minutes every now and then throughout the day simply to consciously breathe and smile. I find this to be a very helpful practice. For it always serves to remind me of my fundamental choice to practice the holy instant, to return to the present moment, to witness my ego and learn that it is not who I am, to reawaken to my connection to the whole of life.

The Smile in All Creation

When I am in my "right mind," when I am centered in my smile, I can see that this smile is everywhere. As I breathe and smile, life smiles back in countless forms. Everything, all of life, holds the smile for me to see and enjoy. And I can begin to recognize that the smile remains even when I'm not mindful of it, even when I forget.

> *In fact, everything around you is keeping your smile for you. You don't need to feel isolated. You only have to open yourself to the support that is all around you, and in you.... You can breathe in awareness, and your smile will return.*
>
> — Thich Nhat Hanh, *Peace Is Every Step*

To say that everything in creation is keeping our smile for us is the same as saying that we can see the presence of God, of love, everywhere. All creation is our family. And the light of God shines in everything.

To be able to look out upon the world with this perception is, perhaps, the fulfillment of all our seeking here. Such seeing is the source of profound gratitude and joy.

> *Life is this simple: we are living in a world that is absolutely transparent and God is shining through it all the time.... God is manifest everywhere, in everything — in people and in things and in nature and in events. God is everywhere and in everything and we cannot be without God. It's simply impossible.*
>
> — Thomas Merton

When we can see love reflected back to us in all things, we understand that we have every reason to smile. We are at home wherever we are. There is nothing to fear.

Peace

Reflect the peace of Heaven here,
and bring this world to Heaven.

—T. p. 272; T-14. X.1:6

The gentle smile is the expression of our commitment to live our human lives in the peace and joy of our spiritual nature. As we find peace within ourselves, we have peace to share with the world.

Peace is the condition for remembrance, for our own awakening and the awakening of the world. Our own peace is perhaps the greatest gift we can give.

If you really knew how to live, what better way to start the day than with a smile? Your smile affirms your awareness and determination to live in peace and joy. How many days slip by in forgetfulness? What are you doing with your life? Look deeply, and smile.

— THICH NHAT HANH, *Present Moment, Wonderful Moment*

The gentle smile of peace is always here, always possible for us to choose. It is as close and as natural to us as our breathing. It is the quiet truth of our own hearts.

In any moment
we can return to ourselves
and remember who we are.
It is as simple — and beautiful —
as a gentle smile.

References

A Course in Miracles. Mill Valley, Calif.: Foundation for Inner Peace, 1975, 1992.

Berends, Polly Berrien. *Coming to Life: Traveling the Spiritual Path in Everyday Life.* San Francisco: HarperCollins, 1990.

Bloch, Douglas. *I Am with You Always.* New York: Bantam Books, 1992.

Borysenko, Joan. *Fire in the Soul: A New Psychology of Spiritual Optimism.* New York: Warner Books, 1993.

———. *Pocketful of Miracles.* New York: Warner Books, 1994.

Canfield, Jack, and Mark Victor Hansen. *Chicken Soup for the Soul.* Deerfield, Fla.: Health Communications, 1993.

Cohen, Alan. *The Dragon Doesn't Live Here Anymore.* New York: Fawcett Columbine (Ballantine Books), 1981, 1990.

Dillard, Annie. *Pilgrim at Tinker Creek.* New York: Harper & Row, 1974.

Fishel, Ruth. *5 Minutes for World Peace...Forever.* Deerfield Beach, Fla.: Health Communications, 1991.

Fox, Matthew. *A Spirituality Named Compassion.* San Francisco: Harper & Row, 1990.

Frankl, Viktor E. *Man's Search for Meaning.* New York: Washington Square Press (Simon & Schuster), 1959, 1962, 1984.

French, Marilyn. *The Women's Room.* New York: Ballantine Books, 1977.

Goldstein, Joseph. *Insight Meditation.* Boston: Shambhala, 1993.

Goldstein, Joseph, and Jack Kornfield. *Seeking the Heart of Wisdom: The Path of Insight Meditation.* Boston: Shambhala, 1987.

Hixon, Lex. *Heart of the Koran.* Wheaton, Ill.: Quest Books (Theosophical Publishing House), 1988.

Kelly, Marcia and Jack, eds. *One Hundred Graces.* New York: Bell Tower, 1992.

Kornfield, Jack. *A Path with Heart: A Guide through the Perils and Promises of Spiritual Life.* New York: Bantam Books, 1993.

Joy, Brugh. *Joy's Way.* Los Angeles: J. P. Tarcher, 1979.

Jung, Carl G. *Man and His Symbols.* New York: Dell, 1964, 1968.

Levine, Stephen. *Healing into Life and Death.* New York: Anchor (Doubleday), 1987.

————. *Guided Meditations, Explorations, and Healings*. New York: Anchor Books (Doubleday), 1991.

Millin, Peggy Tabor. *Mary's Way*. Berkeley, Calif.: Celestial Arts, 1991.

Osho. *Gold Nuggets*. 2d ed. Portland, Ore.: Rebel Publishing Co.

Peace Pilgrim. *Her Life and Work in Her Own Words*. Hemet, Calif.: Friends of Peace Pilgrim, 1982, 1988.

Pema Chodron. *Start Where You Are: A Guide to Compassionate Living*. Boston: Shambhala, 1994.

Praying Their Faith: An Insight into Six World Religions through The Prayers of Their Members. Derby, Eng.: Christian Education Movement, 1992.

Ram Dass and Paul Gorman. *How Can I Help?: Stories and Reflections on Service*. New York: Alfred A. Knopf, 1985, 1993.

Robinson, Jonathan, ed. *Bridges to Heaven: How Well-Known Seekers Define and Deepen Their Connection with God*. Walpole, N.H.: Stillpoint Publishing, 1994.

Sogyal Rinpoche. *The Tibetan Book of Living and Dying*. San Francisco: HarperSanFrancisco, 1993.

Thich Nhat Hanh. *The Miracle of Mindfulness: A Manual on Meditation*. Boston: Beacon Press, 1975, 1976.

————. *Being Peace*. Berkeley, Calif.: Parallax Press, 1987.

————. *Present Moment, Wonderful Moment*. Berkeley, Calif.: Parallax Press, 1990.

————. *Peace Is Every Step: The Path of Mindfulness in Everyday Life*. New York: Bantam Books, 1991.

Trout, Susan. *To See Differently: Personal Growth and Being of Service through Attitudinal Healing*. Washington, D.C.: Three Roses Press, 1990.

Viscott, David. *Finding Your Strength in Difficult Times*. Chicago: Contemporary Books, 1993.

Wapnick, Kenneth. *Glossary-Index for A Course in Miracles*. 3d ed. Roscoe, N.Y.: Foundation for "A Course in Miracles," 1982, 1986, 1989.

Additional Information

On Course, a twice-monthly inspirational magazine published and edited by Jon Mundy and Diane Berke, is available through Interfaith Fellowship. For a sample copy or subscription information, contact: Interfaith Fellowship, 459 Carol Drive, Monroe, NY 10950, (800) 275-4809.

A Course in Miracles may be purchased from the Foundation for Inner Peace, P.O. Box 598, Mill Valley, CA 94942, (415) 388-2060. The three-volume hardcover set is $40. The single volume (all in one) softcover is $25. The hardcover (all in one) is $30.

Diane Berke is, together with Jon Mundy, co-founder and senior minister of Interfaith Fellowship, an alternative, interfaith community of worship in New York City. They also publish the popular inspirational magazine *On Course*. Diane has a private counseling practice in New York City and has taught in the field of personal and spiritual development for nearly fifteen years. She has been a faculty member and dean of training for the New Seminary, which trains and ordains interfaith ministers. Diane is the author of *Love Always Answers: Walking the Path of "Miracles."*

Also by Diane Berke...

Love Always Answers   0-8245-1432-7 $11.95

> "I celebrate Diane Berke's commitment to teaching higher truths. She is a light that illuminates my life."
> —DR. WAYNE DYER, author of *Everyday Wisdom*

By Jon Mundy...

Awaken to Your Own Call   0-8245-1387-8 $11.95

Listening to Your Inner Guide   0-8245-1498-X $13.95

> "I have always felt that Jon Mundy does a wonderful job of explaining *A Course in Miracles*."
> —BEVERLY HUTCHINSON, Miracles Distribution Center

Of related interest...

John Jacob Raub
Who Told You That You Were Naked?   0-8245-1203-0 $10.95

> "A captivatingly simple conversation about a God who always loves and never punishes."
> —WILLIAM SHANNON, author of *Seeking the Face of God*

Ann Tremaine Linthorst
Mothering as a Spiritual Journey   0-8245-1250-2 $11.95

> "As a mother and as a citizen of a very wounded society, I am grateful to her for her voice and its capacity to heal us all."
> —MARIANNE WILLIAMSON, author of *Illuminata*

Please ask for these titles at your book store, or to order directly, send payment (including $3.00 for the first book plus $1.00 for each additional book to cover shipping and handling fees) to: Crossroad, 370 Lexington Avenue, New York, NY 10017.